AI
Self-Driving Cars
Divulgement

Practical Advances in
Artificial Intelligence and Machine Learning

Dr. Lance B. Eliot, MBA, PhD

DEDICATION

To my incredible daughter, Lauren, and my incredible son, Michael.

Forest fortuna adiuvat (from the Latin; good fortune favors the brave).

CONTENTS

Dr. Lance B. Eliot

ACKNOWLEDGMENTS

I have been the beneficiary of advice and counsel by many friends, colleagues, family, investors, and many others. I want to thank everyone that has aided me throughout my career. I write from the heart and the head, having experienced first-hand what it means to have others around you that support you during the good times and the tough times.

To Warren Bennis, one of my doctoral advisors and ultimately a colleague, I offer my deepest thanks and appreciation, especially for his calm and insightful wisdom and support.

To Mark Stevens and his generous efforts toward funding and supporting the USC Stevens Center for Innovation.

To Lloyd Greif and the USC Lloyd Greif Center for Entrepreneurial Studies for their ongoing encouragement of founders and entrepreneurs.

To Peter Drucker, William Wang, Aaron Levie, Peter Kim, Jon Kraft, Cindy Crawford, Jenny Ming, Steve Milligan, Chis Underwood, Frank Gehry, Buzz Aldrin, Steve Forbes, Bill Thompson, Dave Dillon, Alan Fuerstman, Larry Ellison, Jim Sinegal, John Sperling, Mark Stevenson, Anand Nallathambi, Thomas Barrack, Jr., and many other innovators and leaders that I have met and gained mightily from doing so.

Thanks to Ed Trainor, Kevin Anderson, James Hickey, Wendell Jones, Ken Harris, DuWayne Peterson, Mike Brown, Jim Thornton, Abhi Beniwal, Al Biland, John Nomura, Eliot Weinman, John Desmond, and many others for their unwavering support during my career.

And most of all thanks as always to Lauren and Michael, for their ongoing support and for having seen me writing and heard much of this material during the many months involved in writing it. To their patience and willingness to listen.

INTRODUCTION

This is a book that provides the newest innovations and the latest Artificial Intelligence (AI) advances about the emerging nature of AI-based autonomous self-driving driverless cars. Via recent advances in Artificial Intelligence (AI) and Machine Learning (ML), we are nearing the day when vehicles can control themselves and will not require and nor rely upon human intervention to perform their driving tasks (or, that <u>allow</u> for human intervention, but only *require* human intervention in very limited ways).

Similar to my other related books, which I describe in a moment and list the chapters in the Appendix A of this book, I am particularly focused on those advances that pertain to self-driving cars. The phrase "autonomous vehicles" is often used to refer to any kind of vehicle, whether it is ground-based or in the air or sea, and whether it is a cargo hauling trailer truck or a conventional passenger car. Though the aspects described in this book are certainly applicable to all kinds of autonomous vehicles, I am focused more so here on cars.

Indeed, I am especially known for my role in aiding the advancement of self-driving cars, serving currently as the Executive Director of the Cybernetic AI Self-Driving Cars Institute. In addition to writing software, designing and developing systems and software for self-driving cars, I also speak and write quite a bit about the topic. This book is a collection of some of my more advanced essays. For those of you that might have seen my essays posted elsewhere, I have updated them and integrated them into this book as one handy cohesive package.

You might be interested in companion books that I have written that provide additional key innovations and fundamentals about self-driving cars. Those books are entitled **"Introduction to Driverless Self-Driving Cars," "Advances in AI and Autonomous Vehicles: Cybernetic Self-Driving Cars," "Self-Driving Cars: "The Mother of All AI Projects," "Innovation and Thought Leadership on Self-Driving Driverless Cars," "New Advances in AI Autonomous Driverless Self-Driving Cars," "Autonomous Vehicle Driverless Self-Driving Cars and Artificial Intelligence," "Transformative Artificial Intelligence Driverless Self-Driving Cars," "Disruptive Artificial Intelligence and Driverless Self-Driving Cars,** and **"State-of-the-Art AI Driverless Self-Driving Cars,"** and **"Top Trends in AI Self-Driving Cars,"** and **"AI Innovations and Self-Driving Cars," "Crucial Advances for AI**

Driverless Cars," "Sociotechnical Insights and AI Driverless Cars," "Pioneering Advances for AI Driverless Cars" and "Leading Edge Trends for AI Driverless Cars," "The Cutting Edge of AI Autonomous Cars" and "The Next Wave of AI Self-Driving Cars" and "Revolutionary Innovations of AI Self-Driving Cars," and "AI Self-Driving Cars Breakthroughs," "Trailblazing Trends for AI Self-Driving Cars," "Ingenious Strides for AI Driverless Cars," "AI Self-Driving Cars Inventiveness," "Visionary Secrets of AI Driverless Cars," "Spearheading AI Self-Driving Cars," "Spurring AI Self-Driving Cars," "Avant-Garde AI Driverless Cars," "AI Self-Driving Cars Evolvement," "AI Driverless Cars Chrysalis," "Boosting AI Autonomous Cars," "AI Self-Driving Cars Trendsetting," "AI Autonomous Cars Forefront, "AI Autonomous Cars Emergence," "AI Autonomous Cars Progress," "AI Self-Driving Cars Prognosis," "AI Self-Driving Cars Momentum," "AI Self-Driving Cars Headway," "AI Self-Driving Cars Vicissitude," "AI Self-Driving Cars Autonomy," "AI Driverless Cars Transmutation," "AI Driverless Cars Potentiality," "AI Driverless Cars Realities," "AI Self-Driving Cars Materiality, "AI Self-Driving Cars Accordance," "AI Self-Driving Cars Equanimity," "AI Self-Driving Cars Divulgement" (they are available on Amazon).

For this book, I am going to borrow my introduction from those companion books, since it does a good job of laying out the landscape of self-driving cars and my overall viewpoints on the topic.

INTRODUCTION TO SELF-DRIVING CARS

This is a book about self-driving cars. Someday in the future, we'll all have self-driving cars and this book will perhaps seem antiquated, but right now, we are at the forefront of the self-driving car wave. Daily news bombards us with flashes of new announcements by one car maker or another and leaves the impression that within the next few weeks or maybe months that the self-driving car will be here. A casual non-technical reader would assume from these news flashes that in fact we must be on the cusp of a true self-driving car.

We are still quite a distance from having a true self-driving car. A true self-driving car is akin to a moonshot. In the same manner that getting us to the moon was an incredible feat, likewise, is achieving a true self-driving car. Anybody that suggests or even brashly states that the true self-driving car is nearly here should be viewed with great skepticism. Indeed, you'll see that I often tend to use the word "hogwash" or "crock" when I assess much of the decidedly *fake news* about self-driving cars.

Indeed, I've been writing a popular blog post about self-driving cars and hitting hard on those that try to wave their hands and pretend that we are on the imminent verge of true self-driving cars. For many years, I've been known as the AI Insider. Besides writing about AI, I also develop AI software. I do what I describe. It also gives me insights into what others that are doing AI are really doing versus what it is said they are doing.

Many faithful readers had asked me to pull together my insightful short essays and put them into another book, which you are now holding.

For those of you that have been reading my essays over the years, this collection not only puts them together into one handy package, I also updated the essays and added new material. For those of you that are new to the topic of self-driving cars and AI, I hope you find these essays approachable and informative. I also tend to have a writing style with a bit of a voice, and so you'll see that I am times have a wry sense of humor and poke at conformity.

As a former professor and founder of an AI research lab, I for many years wrote in the formal language of academic writing. I published in referred journals and served as an editor for several AI journals. This writing here is not of the nature, and I have adopted a different and more informal style for these essays. That being said, I also do mention from time-to-time more rigorous material on AI and encourage you all to dig into those deeper and more formal materials if so interested.

I am also an AI practitioner. This means that I write AI software for a living. Currently, I head-up the Cybernetics Self-Driving Car Institute, where we are developing AI software for self-driving cars.

For those of you that are reading this book and have a penchant for writing code, you might consider taking a look at the open source code available for self-driving cars. This is a handy place to start learning how to develop AI for self-driving cars. There are also many new educational courses spring forth. There is a growing body of those wanting to learn about and develop self-driving cars, and a growing body of colleges, labs, and other avenues by which you can learn about self-driving cars.

This book will provide a foundation of aspects that I think will get you ready for those kinds of more advanced training opportunities. If you've already taken those classes, you'll likely find these essays especially interesting as they offer a perspective that I am betting few other instructors or faculty offered to you. These are challenging essays that ask you to think beyond the conventional about self-driving cars.

THE MOTHER OF ALL AI PROJECTS

In June 2017, Apple CEO Tim Cook came out and finally admitted that Apple has been working on a self-driving car. As you'll see in my essays, Apple was enmeshed in secrecy about their self-driving car efforts. We have only been able to read the tea leaves and guess at what Apple has been up to. The notion of an iCar has been floating for quite a while, and self-driving engineers and researchers have been signing tight-lipped Non-Disclosure Agreements (NDA's) to work on projects at Apple that were as shrouded in mystery as any military invasion plans might be.

Tim Cook said something that many others in the Artificial Intelligence (AI) field have been saying, namely, the creation of a self-driving car has got to be the mother of all AI projects. In other words, it is in fact a tremendous moonshot for AI. If a self-driving car can be crafted and the AI works as we hope, it means that we have made incredible strides with AI and that therefore it opens many other worlds of potential breakthrough accomplishments that AI can solve.

Is this hyperbole? Am I just trying to make AI seem like a miracle worker and so provide self-aggrandizing statements for those of us writing the AI software for self-driving cars? No, it is not hyperbole. Developing a true self-driving car is really, really, really hard to do. Let me take a moment to explain why. As a side note, I realize that the Apple CEO is known for at times uttering hyperbole, and he had previously said for example that the year 2012 was "the mother of all years," and he had said that the release of iOS 10 was "the mother of all releases" – all of which does suggest he likes to use the handy "mother of" expression. But, I assure you, in terms of true self-driving cars, he has hit the nail on the head. For sure.

When you think about a moonshot and how we got to the moon, there are some identifiable characteristics and those same aspects can be applied to creating a true self-driving car. You'll notice that I keep putting the word "true" in front of the self-driving car expression. I do so because as per my essay about the various levels of self-driving cars, there are some self-driving cars that are only somewhat of a self-driving car. The somewhat versions are ones that require a human driver to be ready to intervene. In my view, that's not a true self-driving car. A true self-driving car is one that requires no human driver intervention at all. It is a car that can entirely undertake via automation the driving task without any human driver needed. This is the essence of what is known as a Level 5 self-driving car. We are currently at the Level 2 and Level 3 mark, and not yet at Level 5.

Getting to the moon involved aspects such as having big stretch goals, incremental progress, experimentation, innovation, and so on. Let's review how this applied to the moonshot of the bygone era, and how it applies to the self-driving car moonshot of today.

Big Stretch Goal

Trying to take a human and deliver the human to the moon, and bring them back, safely, was an extremely large stretch goal at the time. No one knew whether it could be done. The technology wasn't available yet. The cost was huge. The determination would need to be fierce. Etc. To reach a Level 5 self-driving car is going to be the same. It is a big stretch goal. We can readily get to the Level 3, and we are able to see the Level 4 just up ahead, but a Level 5 is still an unknown as to if it is doable. It should eventually be doable and in the same way that we thought we'd eventually get to the moon, but when it will occur is a different story.

Incremental Progress

Getting to the moon did not happen overnight in one fell swoop. It took years and years of incremental progress to get there. Likewise, for self-driving cars. Google has famously been striving to get to the Level 5, and pretty much been willing to forgo dealing with the intervening levels, but most of the other self-driving car makers are doing the incremental route. Let's get a good Level 2 and a somewhat Level 3 going. Then, let's improve the Level 3 and get a somewhat Level 4 going. Then, let's improve the Level 4 and finally arrive at a Level 5. This seems to be the prevalent way that we are going to achieve the true self-driving car.

Experimentation

You likely know that there were various experiments involved in perfecting the approach and technology to get to the moon. As per making incremental progress, we first tried to see if we could get a rocket to go into space and safety return, then put a monkey in there, then with a human, then we went all the way to the moon but didn't land, and finally we arrived at the mission that actually landed on the moon.

Self-driving cars are the same way. We are doing simulations of self-driving cars. We do testing of self-driving cars on private land under controlled situations.

We do testing of self-driving cars on public roadways, often having to meet regulatory requirements including for example having an engineer or equivalent in the car to take over the controls if needed. And so on. Experiments big and small are needed to figure out what works and what doesn't.

Innovation

There are already some advances in AI that are allowing us to progress toward self-driving cars. We are going to need even more advances. Innovation in all aspects of technology are going to be required to achieve a true self-driving car. By no means do we already have everything in-hand that we need to get there. Expect new inventions and new approaches, new algorithms, etc.

Setbacks

Most of the pundits are avoiding talking about potential setbacks in the progress toward self-driving cars. Getting to the moon involved many setbacks, some of which you never have heard of and were buried at the time so as to not dampen enthusiasm and funding for getting to the moon. A recurring theme in many of my included essays is that there are going to be setbacks as we try to arrive at a true self-driving car. Take a deep breath and be ready. I just hope the setbacks don't completely stop progress. I am sure that it will cause progress to alter in a manner that we've not yet seen in the self-driving car field. I liken the self-driving car of today to the excitement everyone had for Uber when it first got going. Today, we have a different view of Uber and with each passing day there are more regulations to the ride sharing business and more concerns raised. The darling child only stays a darling until finally that child acts up. It will happen the same with self-driving cars.

SELF-DRIVING CARS CHALLENGES

But what exactly makes things so hard to have a true self-driving car, you might be asking. You have seen cruise control for years and years. You've lately seen cars that can do parallel parking. You've seen YouTube videos of Tesla drivers that put their hands out the window as their car zooms along the highway, and seen to therefore be in a self-driving car. Aren't we just needing to put a few more sensors onto a car and then we'll have in-hand a true self-driving car? Nope.

Consider for a moment the nature of the driving task. We don't just let anyone at any age drive a car. Worldwide, most countries won't license a driver until the age of 18, though many do allow a learner's permit at the age of 15 or 16. Some suggest that a younger age would be physically too small to reach the controls of the car. Though this might be the case, we could easily adjust the controls to allow for younger aged and thus smaller stature. It's not their physical size that matters. It's their cognitive development that matters.

To drive a car, you need to be able to reason about the car, what the car can and cannot do. You need to know how to operate the car. You need to know about how other cars on the road drive. You need to know what is allowed in driving such as speed limits and driving within marked lanes. You need to be able to react to situations and be able to avoid getting into accidents. You need to ascertain when to hit your brakes, when to steer clear of a pedestrian, and how to keep from ramming that motorcyclist that just cut you off.

Many of us had taken courses on driving. We studied about driving and took driver training. We had to take a test and pass it to be able to drive. The point being that though most adults take the driving task for granted, and we often "mindlessly" drive our cars, there is a significant amount of cognitive effort that goes into driving a car. After a while, it becomes second nature. You don't especially think about how you drive, you just do it. But, if you watch a novice driver, say a teenager learning to drive, you suddenly realize that there is a lot more complexity to it than we seem to realize.

Furthermore, driving is a very serious task. I recall when my daughter and son first learned to drive. They are both very conscientious people. They wanted to make sure that whatever they did, they did well, and that they did not harm anyone. Every day, when you get into a car, it is probably around 4,000 pounds of hefty metal and plastics (about two tons), and it is a lethal weapon. Think about it. You drive down the street in an object that weighs two tons and with the engine it can accelerate and ram into anything you want to hit. The damage a car can inflict is very scary. Both my children were surprised that they were being given the right to maneuver this monster of a beast that could cause tremendous harm entirely by merely letting go of the steering wheel for a moment or taking your eyes off the road.

In fact, in the United States alone there are about 30,000 deaths per year by auto accidents, which is around 100 per day. Given that there are about 263 million cars in the United States, I am actually more amazed that the number of fatalities is not a lot higher.

During my morning commute, I look at all the thousands of cars on the freeway around me, and I think that if all of them decided to go zombie and drive in a crazy maniac way, there would be many people dead. Somehow, incredibly, each day, most people drive relatively safely. To me, that's a miracle right there. Getting millions and millions of people to be safe and sane when behind the wheel of a two-ton mobile object, it's a feat that we as a society should admire with pride.

So, hopefully you are in agreement that the driving task requires a great deal of cognition. You don't' need to be especially smart to drive a car, and we've done quite a bit to make car driving viable for even the average dolt. There isn't an IQ test that you need to take to drive a car. If you can read and write, and pass a test, you pretty much can legally drive a car. There are of course some that drive a car and are not legally permitted to do so, plus there are private areas such as farms where drivers are young, but for public roadways in the United States, you can be generally of average intelligence (or less) and be able to legally drive.

This though makes it seem like the cognitive effort must not be much. If the cognitive effort was truly hard, wouldn't we only have Einstein's that could drive a car? We have made sure to keep the driving task as simple as we can, by making the controls easy and relatively standardized, and by having roads that are relatively standardized, and so on. It is as though Disneyland has put their Autopia into the real-world, by us all as a society agreeing that roads will be a certain way, and we'll all abide by the various rules of driving.

A modest cognitive task by a human is still something that stymies AI. You certainly know that AI has been able to beat chess players and be good at other kinds of games. This type of narrow cognition is not what car driving is about. Car driving is much wider. It requires knowledge about the world, which a chess playing AI system does not need to know. The cognitive aspects of driving are on the one hand seemingly simple, but at the same time require layer upon layer of knowledge about cars, people, roads, rules, and a myriad of other "common sense" aspects. We don't have any AI systems today that have that same kind of breadth and depth of awareness and knowledge.

As revealed in my essays, the self-driving car of today is using trickery to do particular tasks. It is all very narrow in operation. Plus, it currently assumes that a human driver is ready to intervene. It is like a child that we have taught to stack blocks, but we are needed to be right there in case the child stacks them too high and they begin to fall over.

AI of today is brittle, it is narrow, and it does not approach the cognitive abilities of humans. This is why the true self-driving car is somewhere out in the future.

Another aspect to the driving task is that it is not solely a mind exercise. You do need to use your senses to drive. You use your eyes as vision sensors to see the road ahead. You vision capability is like a streaming video, which your brain needs to continually analyze as you drive. Where is the road? Is there a pedestrian in the way? Is there another car ahead of you? Your senses are relying a flood of info to your brain. Self-driving cars are trying to do the same, by using cameras, radar, ultrasound, and lasers. This is an attempt at mimicking how humans have senses and sensory apparatus.

Thus, the driving task is mental and physical. You use your senses, you use your arms and legs to manipulate the controls of the car, and you use your brain to assess the sensory info and direct your limbs to act upon the controls of the car. This all happens instantly. If you've ever perhaps gotten something in your eye and only had one eye available to drive with, you suddenly realize how dependent upon vision you are. If you have a broken foot with a cast, you suddenly realize how hard it is to control the brake pedal and the accelerator. If you've taken medication and your brain is maybe sluggish, you suddenly realize how much mental strain is required to drive a car.

An AI system that plays chess only needs to be focused on playing chess. The physical aspects aren't important because usually a human moves the chess pieces or the chessboard is shown on an electronic display. Using AI for a more life-and-death task such as analyzing MRI images of patients, this again does not require physical capabilities and instead is done by examining images of bits.

Driving a car is a true life-and-death task. It is a use of AI that can easily and at any moment produce death. For those colleagues of mine that are developing this AI, as am I, we need to keep in mind the somber aspects of this. We are producing software that will have in its virtual hands the lives of the occupants of the car, and the lives of those in other nearby cars, and the lives of nearby pedestrians, etc. Chess is not usually a life-or-death matter.

Driving is all around us. Cars are everywhere. Most of today's AI applications involve only a small number of people. Or, they are behind the scenes and we as humans have other recourse if the AI messes up. AI that is driving a car at 80 miles per hour on a highway had better not mess up. The consequences are grave.

Multiply this by the number of cars, if we could put magically self-driving into every car in the USA, we'd have AI running in the 263 million cars. That's a lot of AI spread around. This is AI on a massive scale that we are not doing today and that offers both promise and potential peril.

There are some that want AI for self-driving cars because they envision a world without any car accidents. They envision a world in which there is no car congestion and all cars cooperate with each other. These are wonderful utopian visions.

They are also very misleading. The adoption of self-driving cars is going to be incremental and not overnight. We cannot economically just junk all existing cars. Nor are we going to be able to affordably retrofit existing cars. It is more likely that self-driving cars will be built into new cars and that over many years of gradual replacement of existing cars that we'll see the mix of self-driving cars become substantial in the real-world.

In these essays, I have tried to offer technological insights without being overly technical in my description, and also blended the business, societal, and economic aspects too. Technologists need to consider the non-technological impacts of what they do. Non-technologists should be aware of what is being developed.

We all need to work together to collectively be prepared for the enormous disruption and transformative aspects of true self-driving cars.

WHAT THIS BOOK PROVIDES

What does this book provide to you? It introduces many of the key elements about self-driving cars and does so with an AI based perspective. I weave together technical and non-technical aspects, readily going from being concerned about the cognitive capabilities of the driving task and how the technology is embodying this into self-driving cars, and in the next breath I discuss the societal and economic aspects.

They are all intertwined because that's the way reality is. You cannot separate out the technology per se, and instead must consider it within the milieu of what is being invented and innovated, and do so with a mindset towards the contemporary mores and culture that shape what we are doing and what we hope to do.

WHY THIS BOOK

I wrote this book to try and bring to the public view many aspects about self-driving cars that nobody seems to be discussing.

For business leaders that are either involved in making self-driving cars or that are going to leverage self-driving cars, I hope that this book will enlighten you as to the risks involved and ways in which you should be strategizing about how to deal with those risks.

For entrepreneurs, startups and other businesses that want to enter into the self-driving car market that is emerging, I hope this book sparks your interest in doing so, and provides some sense of what might be prudent to pursue.

For researchers that study self-driving cars, I hope this book spurs your interest in the risks and safety issues of self-driving cars, and also nudges you toward conducting research on those aspects.

For students in computer science or related disciplines, I hope this book will provide you with interesting and new ideas and material, for which you might conduct research or provide some career direction insights for you.

For AI companies and high-tech companies pursuing self-driving cars, this book will hopefully broaden your view beyond just the mere coding and development needed to make self-driving cars.

For all readers, I hope that you will find the material in this book to be stimulating. Some of it will be repetitive of things you already know. But I am pretty sure that you'll also find various eureka moments whereby you'll discover a new technique or approach that you had not earlier thought of. I am also betting that there will be material that forces you to rethink some of your current practices.

I am not saying you will suddenly have an epiphany and change what you are doing. I do think though that you will reconsider or perhaps revisit what you are doing.

For anyone choosing to use this book for teaching purposes, please take a look at my suggestions for doing so, as described in the Appendix. I have found the material handy in courses that I have taught, and likewise other faculty have told me that they have found the material handy, in some cases as extended readings and in other instances as a core part of their course (depending on the nature of the class).

In my writing for this book, I have tried carefully to blend both the practitioner and the academic styles of writing.

It is not as abstract as is typical academic journal writing, but at the same time offers depth by going into the nuances and trade-offs of various practices.

The word "deep" is in vogue today, meaning getting deeply into a subject or topic, and so is the word "unpack" which means to tease out the underlying aspects of a subject or topic. I have sought to offer material that addresses an issue or topic by going relatively deeply into it and make sure that it is well unpacked.

In any book about AI, it is difficult to use our everyday words without having some of them be misinterpreted. Specifically, it is easy to anthropomorphize AI. When I say that an AI system "knows" something, I do not want you to construe that the AI system has sentience and "knows" in the same way that humans do. They aren't that way, as yet. I have tried to use quotes around such words from time-to-time to emphasize that the words I am using should not be misinterpreted to ascribe true human intelligence to the AI systems that we know of today. If I used quotes around all such words, the book would be very difficult to read, and so I am doing so judiciously. Please keep that in mind as you read the material, thanks.

Some of the material is time-based in terms of covering underway activities, and though some of it might decay, nonetheless I believe you'll find the material useful and informative.

COMPANION BOOKS BY DR. ELIOT

1. **"Introduction to Driverless Self-Driving Cars"** by Dr. Lance Eliot
2. **"Innovation and Thought Leadership on Self-Driving Driverless Cars"**
3. **"Advances in AI and Autonomous Vehicles: Cybernetic Self-Driving Cars"**
4. **"Self-Driving Cars: The Mother of All AI Projects"** by Dr. Lance Eliot
5. **"New Advances in AI Autonomous Driverless Self-Driving Cars"**
6. **"Autonomous Vehicle Driverless Self-Driving Cars and Artificial Intelligence"** by Dr. Lance Eliot and Michael B. Eliot
7. **"Transformative Artificial Intelligence Driverless Self-Driving Cars"**
8. **"Disruptive Artificial Intelligence and Driverless Self-Driving Cars"**
9. "State-of-the-Art AI Driverless Self-Driving Cars" by Dr. Lance Eliot
10. **"Top Trends in AI Self-Driving Cars"** by Dr. Lance Eliot
11. **"AI Innovations and Self-Driving Cars"** by Dr. Lance Eliot
12. **"Crucial Advances for AI Driverless Cars"** by Dr. Lance Eliot
13. **"Sociotechnical Insights and AI Driverless Cars"** by Dr. Lance Eliot.
14. **"Pioneering Advances for AI Driverless Cars"** by Dr. Lance Eliot
15. **"Leading Edge Trends for AI Driverless Cars"** by Dr. Lance Eliot
16. **"The Cutting Edge of AI Autonomous Cars"** by Dr. Lance Eliot
17. **"The Next Wave of AI Self-Driving Cars"** by Dr. Lance Eliot
18. **"Revolutionary Innovations of AI Driverless Cars"** by Dr. Lance Eliot
19. **"AI Self-Driving Cars Breakthroughs"** by Dr. Lance Eliot
20. **"Trailblazing Trends for AI Self-Driving Cars"** by Dr. Lance Eliot
21. **"Ingenious Strides for AI Driverless Cars"** by Dr. Lance Eliot
22. **"AI Self-Driving Cars Inventiveness"** by Dr. Lance Eliot
23. **"Visionary Secrets of AI Driverless Cars"** by Dr. Lance Eliot
24. **"Spearheading AI Self-Driving Cars"** by Dr. Lance Eliot
25. **"Spurring AI Self-Driving Cars"** by Dr. Lance Eliot
26. **"Avant-Garde AI Driverless Cars"** by Dr. Lance Eliot
27. **"AI Self-Driving Cars Evolvement"** by Dr. Lance Eliot
28. **"AI Driverless Cars Chrysalis"** by Dr. Lance Eliot
29. **"Boosting AI Autonomous Cars"** by Dr. Lance Eliot
30. **"AI Self-Driving Cars Trendsetting"** by Dr. Lance Eliot
31. **"AI Autonomous Cars Forefront"** by Dr. Lance Eliot
32. **"AI Autonomous Cars Emergence"** by Dr. Lance Eliot
33. **"AI Autonomous Cars Progress"** by Dr. Lance Eliot
34. **"AI Self-Driving Cars Prognosis"** by Dr. Lance Eliot
35. **"AI Self-Driving Cars Momentum"** by Dr. Lance Eliot
36. **"AI Self-Driving Cars Headway"** by Dr. Lance Eliot
37. **"AI Self-Driving Cars Vicissitude"** by Dr. Lance Eliot
38. **"AI Self-Driving Cars Autonomy"** by Dr. Lance Eliot
39. **"AI Driverless Cars Transmutation"** by Dr. Lance Eliot
40. **"AI Driverless Cars Potentiality"** by Dr. Lance Eliot
41. **"AI Driverless Cars Realities"** by Dr. Lance Eliot
42. **"AI Self-Driving Cars Materiality"** by Dr. Lance Eliot
43. **"AI Self-Driving Cars Accordance"** by Dr. Lance Eliot
44. **"AI Self-Driving Cars Equanimity"** by Dr. Lance Eliot
45. **"AI Self-Driving Cars Divulgement"** by Dr. Lance Eliot

These books are available on Amazon and at other major global booksellers.

CHAPTER 1

ELIOT FRAMEWORK FOR AI SELF-DRIVING CARS

CHAPTER 1

ELIOT FRAMEWORK FOR AI SELF-DRIVING CARS

This chapter is a core foundational aspect for understanding AI self-driving cars and I have used this same chapter in several of my other books to introduce the reader to essential elements of this field. Once you've read this chapter, you'll be prepared to read the rest of the material since the foundational essence of the components of autonomous AI driverless self-driving cars will have been established for you.

———————

When I give presentations about self-driving cars and teach classes on the topic, I have found it helpful to provide a framework around which the various key elements of self-driving cars can be understood and organized (see diagram at the end of this chapter). The framework needs to be simple enough to convey the overarching elements, but at the same time not so simple that it belies the true complexity of self-driving cars. As such, I am going to describe the framework here and try to offer in a thousand words (or more!) what the framework diagram itself intends to portray.

The core elements on the diagram are numbered for ease of reference. The numbering does not suggest any kind of prioritization of the elements. Each element is crucial. Each element has a purpose, and otherwise would not be included in the framework. For some self-driving cars, a particular element might be more important or somehow distinguished in comparison to other self-driving cars.

You could even use the framework to rate a particular self-driving car, doing so by gauging how well it performs in each of the elements of the framework. I will describe each of the elements, one at a time. After doing so, I'll discuss aspects that illustrate how the elements interact and perform during the overall effort of a self-driving car.

At the AI Self-Driving Car Institute, we use the framework to keep track of what we are working on, and how we are developing software that fills in what is needed to achieve Level 5 self-driving cars.

D-01: Sensor Capture

Let's start with the one element that often gets the most attention in the press about self-driving cars, namely, the sensory devices for a self-driving car.

On the framework, the box labeled as D-01 indicates "Sensor Capture" and refers to the processes of the self-driving car that involve collecting data from the myriad of sensors that are used for a self-driving car. The types of devices typically involved are listed, such as the use of mono cameras, stereo cameras, LIDAR devices, radar systems, ultrasonic devices, GPS, IMU, and so on.

These devices are tasked with obtaining data about the status of the self-driving car and the world around it. Some of the devices are continually providing updates, while others of the devices await an indication by the self-driving car that the device is supposed to collect data. The data might be first transformed in some fashion by the device itself, or it might instead be fed directly into the sensor capture as raw data. At that point, it might be up to the sensor capture processes to do transformations on the data. This all varies depending upon the nature of the devices being used and how the devices were designed and developed.

D-02: Sensor Fusion

Imagine that your eyeballs receive visual images, your nose receives odors, your ears receive sounds, and in essence each of your distinct sensory devices is getting some form of input. The input befits the nature of the device. Likewise, for a self-driving car, the cameras provide visual images, the radar returns radar reflections, and so on. Each device provides the data as befits what the device does.

At some point, using the analogy to humans, you need to merge together what your eyes see, what your nose smells, what your ears hear, and piece it all together into a larger sense of what the world is all about and what is happening around you. Sensor fusion is the action of taking the singular aspects from each of the devices and putting them together into a larger puzzle.

Sensor fusion is a tough task. There are some devices that might not be working at the time of the sensor capture. Or, there might some devices that are unable to report well what they have detected. Again, using a human analogy, suppose you are in a dark room and so your eyes cannot see much. At that point, you might need to rely more so on your ears and what you hear. The same is true for a self-driving car. If the cameras are obscured due to snow and sleet, it might be that the radar can provide a greater indication of what the external conditions consist of.

In the case of a self-driving car, there can be a plethora of such sensory devices. Each is reporting what it can. Each might have its difficulties. Each might have its limitations, such as how far ahead it can detect an object. All of these limitations need to be considered during the sensor fusion task.

D-03: Virtual World Model

For humans, we presumably keep in our minds a model of the world around us when we are driving a car. In your mind, you know that the car is going at say 60 miles per hour and that you are on a freeway.

You have a model in your mind that your car is surrounded by other cars, and that there are lanes to the freeway. Your model is not only based on what you can see, hear, etc., but also what you know about the nature of the world. You know that at any moment that car ahead of you can smash on its brakes, or the car behind you can ram into your car, or that the truck in the next lane might swerve into your lane.

The AI of the self-driving car needs to have a virtual world model, which it then keeps updated with whatever it is receiving from the sensor fusion, which received its input from the sensor capture and the sensory devices.

D-04: System Action Plan

By having a virtual world model, the AI of the self-driving car is able to keep track of where the car is and what is happening around the car. In addition, the AI needs to determine what to do next. Should the self-driving car hit its brakes? Should the self-driving car stay in its lane or swerve into the lane to the left? Should the self-driving car accelerate or slow down?

A system action plan needs to be prepared by the AI of the self-driving car. The action plan specifies what actions should be taken. The actions need to pertain to the status of the virtual world model. Plus, the actions need to be realizable.

This realizability means that the AI cannot just assert that the self-driving car should suddenly sprout wings and fly. Instead, the AI must be bound by whatever the self-driving car can actually do, such as coming to a halt in a distance of X feet at a speed of Y miles per hour, rather than perhaps asserting that the self-driving car come to a halt in 0 feet as though it could instantaneously come to a stop while it is in motion.

D-05: Controls Activation

The system action plan is implemented by activating the controls of the car to act according to what the plan stipulates.

This might mean that the accelerator control is commanded to increase the speed of the car. Or, the steering control is commanded to turn the steering wheel 30 degrees to the left or right.

One question arises as to whether or not the controls respond as they are commanded to do. In other words, suppose the AI has commanded the accelerator to increase, but for some reason it does not do so. Or, maybe it tries to do so, but the speed of the car does not increase. The controls activation feeds back into the virtual world model, and simultaneously the virtual world model is getting updated from the sensors, the sensor capture, and the sensor fusion. This allows the AI to ascertain what has taken place as a result of the controls being commanded to take some kind of action.

By the way, please keep in mind that though the diagram seems to have a linear progression to it, the reality is that these are all aspects of the self-driving car that are happening in parallel and simultaneously. The sensors are capturing data, meanwhile the sensor fusion is taking place, meanwhile the virtual model is being updated, meanwhile the system action plan is being formulated and reformulated, meanwhile the controls are being activated.

This is the same as a human being that is driving a car. They are eyeballing the road, meanwhile they are fusing in their mind the sights, sounds, etc., meanwhile their mind is updating their model of the world around them, meanwhile they are formulating an action plan of what to do, and meanwhile they are pushing their foot onto the pedals and steering the car. In the normal course of driving a car, you are doing all of these at once. I mention this so that when you look at the diagram, you will think of the boxes as processes that are all happening at the same time, and not as though only one happens and then the next.

They are shown diagrammatically in a simplistic manner to help comprehend what is taking place. You though should also realize that they are working in parallel and simultaneous with each other. This is a tough aspect in that the inter-element communications involve latency and other aspects that must be taken into account.

There can be delays in one element updating and then sharing its latest status with other elements.

D-06: Automobile & CAN

Contemporary cars use various automotive electronics and a Controller Area Network (CAN) to serve as the components that underlie the driving aspects of a car. There are Electronic Control Units (ECU's) which control subsystems of the car, such as the engine, the brakes, the doors, the windows, and so on.

The elements D-01, D-02, D-03, D-04, D-05 are layered on top of the D-06, and must be aware of the nature of what the D-06 is able to do and not do.

D-07: In-Car Commands

Humans are going to be occupants in self-driving cars. In a Level 5 self-driving car, there must be some form of communication that takes place between the humans and the self-driving car. For example, I go into a self-driving car and tell it that I want to be driven over to Disneyland, and along the way I want to stop at In-and-Out Burger. The self-driving car now parses what I've said and tries to then establish a means to carry out my wishes.

In-car commands can happen at any time during a driving journey. Though my example was about an in-car command when I first got into my self-driving car, it could be that while the self-driving car is carrying out the journey that I change my mind. Perhaps after getting stuck in traffic, I tell the self-driving car to forget about getting the burgers and just head straight over to the theme park. The self-driving car needs to be alert to in-car commands throughout the journey.

D-08: V2X Communications

We will ultimately have self-driving cars communicating with each other, doing so via V2V (Vehicle-to-Vehicle) communications.

We will also have self-driving cars that communicate with the roadways and other aspects of the transportation infrastructure, doing so via V2I (Vehicle-to-Infrastructure).

The variety of ways in which a self-driving car will be communicating with other cars and infrastructure is being called V2X, whereby the letter X means whatever else we identify as something that a car should or would want to communicate with. The V2X communications will be taking place simultaneous with everything else on the diagram, and those other elements will need to incorporate whatever it gleans from those V2X communications.

D-09: Deep Learning

The use of Deep Learning permeates all other aspects of the self-driving car. The AI of the self-driving car will be using deep learning to do a better job at the systems action plan, and at the control's activation, and at the sensor fusion, and so on.

Currently, the use of artificial neural networks is the most prevalent form of deep learning. Based on large swaths of data, the neural networks attempt to "learn" from the data and therefore direct the efforts of the self-driving car accordingly.

D-10: Tactical AI

Tactical AI is the element of dealing with the moment-to-moment driving of the self-driving car. Is the self-driving car staying in its lane of the freeway? Is the car responding appropriately to the controls commands? Are the sensory devices working?

For human drivers, the tactical equivalent can be seen when you watch a novice driver such as a teenager that is first driving. They are focused on the mechanics of the driving task, keeping their eye on the road while also trying to properly control the car.

D-11: Strategic AI

The Strategic AI aspects of a self-driving car are dealing with the larger picture of what the self-driving car is trying to do. If I had asked that the self-driving car take me to Disneyland, there is an overall journey map that needs to be kept and maintained.

There is an interaction between the Strategic AI and the Tactical AI. The Strategic AI is wanting to keep on the mission of the driving, while the Tactical AI is focused on the particulars underway in the driving effort. If the Tactical AI seems to wander away from the overarching mission, the Strategic AI wants to see why and get things back on track. If the Tactical AI realizes that there is something amiss on the self-driving car, it needs to alert the Strategic AI accordingly and have an adjustment to the overarching mission that is underway.

D-12: Self-Aware AI

Very few of the self-driving cars being developed are including a Self-Aware AI element, which we at the Cybernetic Self-Driving Car Institute believe is crucial to Level 5 self-driving cars.

The Self-Aware AI element is intended to watch over itself, in the sense that the AI is making sure that the AI is working as intended. Suppose you had a human driving a car, and they were starting to drive erratically. Hopefully, their own self-awareness would make them realize they themselves are driving poorly, such as perhaps starting to fall asleep after having been driving for hours on end. If you had a passenger in the car, they might be able to alert the driver if the driver is starting to do something amiss.

This is exactly what the Self-Aware AI element tries to do, it becomes the overseer of the AI, and tries to detect when the AI has become faulty or confused, and then find ways to overcome the issue.

D-13: Economic

The economic aspects of a self-driving car are not per se a technology aspect of a self-driving car, but the economics do indeed impact the nature of a self-driving car. For example, the cost of outfitting a self-driving car with every kind of possible sensory device is prohibitive, and so choices need to be made about which devices are used. And, for those sensory devices chosen, whether they would have a full set of features or a more limited set of features.

We are going to have self-driving cars that are at the low-end of a consumer cost point, and others at the high-end of a consumer cost point. You cannot expect that the self-driving car at the low-end is going to be as robust as the one at the high-end. I realize that many of the self-driving car pundits are acting as though all self-driving cars will be the same, but they won't be. Just like anything else, we are going to have self-driving cars that have a range of capabilities. Some will be better than others. Some will be safer than others. This is the way of the real-world, and so we need to be thinking about the economics aspects when considering the nature of self-driving cars.

D-14: Societal

This component encompasses the societal aspects of AI which also impacts the technology of self-driving cars. For example, the famous Trolley Problem involves what choices should a self-driving car make when faced with life-and-death matters. If the self-driving car is about to either hit a child standing in the roadway, or instead ram into a tree at the side of the road and possibly kill the humans in the self-driving car, which choice should be made?

We need to keep in mind the societal aspects will underlie the AI of the self-driving car. Whether we are aware of it explicitly or not, the AI will have embedded into it various societal assumptions.

D-15: Innovation

I included the notion of innovation into the framework because we can anticipate that whatever a self-driving car consists of, it will continue to be innovated over time. The self-driving cars coming out in the next several years will undoubtedly be different and less innovative than the versions that come out in ten years hence, and so on.

Framework Overall

For those of you that want to learn about self-driving cars, you can potentially pick a particular element and become specialized in that aspect. Some engineers are focusing on the sensory devices. Some engineers focus on the controls activation. And so on. There are specialties in each of the elements.

Researchers are likewise specializing in various aspects. For example, there are researchers that are using Deep Learning to see how best it can be used for sensor fusion. There are other researchers that are using Deep Learning to derive good System Action Plans. Some are studying how to develop AI for the Strategic aspects of the driving task, while others are focused on the Tactical aspects.

A well-prepared all-around software developer that is involved in self-driving cars should be familiar with all of the elements, at least to the degree that they know what each element does. This is important since whatever piece of the pie that the software developer works on, they need to be knowledgeable about what the other elements are doing.

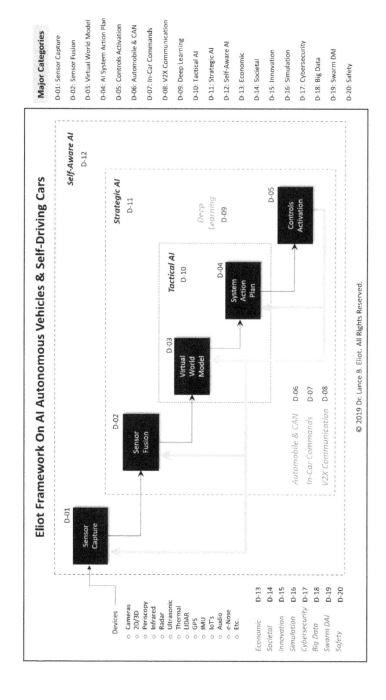

Eliot Framework On AI Autonomous Vehicles & Self-Driving Cars

Major Categories

D-01: Sensor Capture
D-02: Sensor Fusion
D-03: Virtual World Model
D-04: AI System Action Plan
D-05: Controls Activation
D-06: Automobile & CAN
D-07: In-Car Commands
D-08: V2X Communication
D-09: Deep Learning
D-10: Tactical AI
D-11: Strategic AI
D-12: Self-Aware AI
D-13: Economic
D-14: Societal
D-15: Innovation
D-16: Simulation
D-17: Cybersecurity
D-18: Big Data
D-19: Swarm DAI
D-20: Safety

CHAPTER 2
DISCOVERING INTELLIGENT LIFE AND AI SELF-DRIVING CARS

CHAPTER 2

DISCOVERING INTELLIGENT LIFE AND AI SELF-DRIVING CARS

Is there intelligent life beyond our planet?

Nobody here knows, though there are plenty of efforts to find out.

The Search for Extraterrestrial Intelligence (SETI) has been going on for many years.

The most common means for conducting the search consists of examining electromagnetic pulses coming from outer space. By intercepting such pulses as they are radiating across space, we hope to spot anything that might be a telltale clue of intelligent life that is beaming out those rays.

It could be that some intelligent creatures are purposely trying to send us a message, doing so from far away, and they are hoping that we are astute enough to detect the messages. In that sense, the communique could be a purposeful one.

Or, it might be that there are intelligent creatures that are doing things for which electromagnetic exhaust or spillover is occurring.

In that case, we might get lucky and detect the leakage, remarkably discovering the intelligent life and yet perhaps it has not yet discovered us (I'm going to be generous and state that we are indeed intelligent life too if you get my drift).

What are the odds of making such an incredible discovery?

You might have heard of the famous Drake equation, a formula that was devised in the early 1960s by scientist Frank Drake to help estimate the odds of their being intelligent life in our galaxy. His equation is relatively simple and yet powerful enough to have been long-lasting. Many have expanded upon his equation or have criticized elements of it.

In any case, he had tried to estimate the odds that there are detectable civilizations in the Milky Way galaxy.

By monitoring narrow-bandwidth radio signals and doing copious analysis of the signals, maybe we can ferret out that intelligent life is close to home (somewhere in our own galaxy). Various scientists have played with Drake's equation and some say that the probability of there being other intelligent life in our galaxy and that we are able to detect them is near to zero (so close to zero that we should assume it is zero), while others claim that it is definitely a non-zero chance and we have a "reasonable" basis to keep looking.

We can continue to look even if the odds are slim.

People are looking for various reasons.

One reason is out of pure curiosity. Another is that if there is intelligent life, maybe we can learn something from them that will help us. Yet another reason is the sci-fi portrayal that maybe an intelligent life will ultimately come to take over our planet, and thus we ought to find them before they start their invasion.

As part of the search, computers can be used to examine the radio signals coming from outer space that scientists are in the process of collecting. It is a tedious effort by computers and involves mathematically looking for patterns within the radio signals.

By-and-large, the radio waves are just noise, random bits of this or that, and the assumption is that if there a distinct pattern within the signals, it could mean that those are emanating as a purposeful signal or a spillover signal.

Supercomputers of massive computational capability have been and are continuing to be used to examine the voluminous radio signal data. It is a never-ending task.

Years ago, some realized that it might be possible to harness everyday PC's or people's home microcomputers to also aid in the electronic hunt. A screen saver program was developed that could be easily loaded onto a PC and be used as a participant in the search. Essentially, via the Internet, chunks of the radio signal data could be downloaded to a PC, the PC would crunch away, and then the PC would report its results.

If you could get lots and lots of PC's doing this, and if you carefully coordinated the data being parceled out, you could do as much or even more than a single supercomputer could do.

Some liken this to the democratization of the search for intelligent life, while others say it is merely a practical way to leverage the millions upon millions of everyday desktop and laptop computers that now exist on our planet.

Those that download and employ the software are willingly allowing their computers to be used in the search effort. Much of the time your computer is likely idle and has nothing especially important to do.

Why not let it participate in a larger than life kind of effort, quietly aiming to discover intelligent life beyond our borders?

You might say that you don't want to know whether there is other intelligent life, and therefore decide to not be part of the search.

Or, you might not want your computer to be used for anything other than for your own purposes.

Those that relish conspiracy theories are apt to even believe that if their computer happens to be the one that detects intelligent life, those intelligent beings might decide that the owner of that computer is the first to go. Yikes, you could have done yourself in by simply participating in the search (well, this seems kind of a wacky notion, but everyone has their own cup of tea).

For those of you that are interested in participating in the search, you can potentially make use of SETI@home, which has been based at the University of California Berkeley, though recently they decided to halt the distribution of the home version of the software. Via the SETI@home downloadable program, which was free of charge, you could install software that analyzes radio telescope data and report the results of the analysis.

When I say free of charge, realize that you need to have access to the Internet, which you are probably paying for already, and you are allowing your computer to work on the data, thus the computer needs to be powered on (incurring presumably electricity, which you are likely paying to use). Thus, there are some costs associated with your aiding the effort (e.g., your Internet access, your power consumption, your computer cycles), but it's probably a negligible cost overall for you.

Here's an intriguing question: *Could the advent of true self-driving cars potentially help us in the search for discovering intelligent life on other planets?*

My answer is yes.

Let's unpack the matter and see why.

The Levels Of Self-Driving Cars

It is important to clarify what I mean when referring to true self-driving cars.

True self-driving cars are ones that the AI drives the car entirely on its own and there isn't any human assistance during the driving task.

These driverless cars are considered a Level 4 and Level 5, while a car that requires a human driver to co-share the driving effort is usually considered at a Level 2 or Level 3. The cars that co-share the driving task are described as being semi-autonomous, and typically contain a variety of automated add-ons that are referred to as ADAS (Advanced Driver-Assistance Systems).

There is not yet a true self-driving car at Level 5, which we don't yet even know if this will be possible to achieve, and nor how long it will take to get there.

Meanwhile, the Level 4 efforts are gradually trying to get some traction by undergoing very narrow and selective public roadway trials, though there is controversy over whether this testing should be allowed per se (we are all life-or-death guinea pigs in an experiment taking place on our highways and byways, some point out).

Since semi-autonomous cars require a human driver, computer processing capabilities are typically less powerful than the computers used on truly autonomous cars. As will be explained shortly, the powerful computers employed in self-driving cars will be the key to the suggestion that driverless cars can help find intelligent life outside of our planet.

For semi-autonomous cars, it is important that I mention a disconcerting aspect, namely that in spite of those human drivers that keep posting videos of themselves falling asleep at the wheel of a Level 2 or Level 3 car, do not be misled into believing that you can take away your attention from the driving task while driving a semi-autonomous car.

You are the responsible party for the driving actions of the car, regardless of how much automation might be tossed into a Level 2 or Level 3.

Self-Driving Cars And The Search For Intelligent Life

For Level 4 and Level 5 true self-driving cars, since they are going to be equipped with quite powerful computers, we can consider how those driverless cars can be an aid in the search for intelligent life.

The AI software will be running on the on-board computers and has the life-or-death role of driving the car.

There isn't a human driving the car.

All the occupants inside a self-driving car are passengers.

While a self-driving car is in motion, the AI is churning away and examining the sensory data to figure out what the driving scene consists of. The AI must interpret the data and make "decisions" about what the car should do next. This is a computationally intensive task and requires some rather impressive computing capabilities to be included in the driverless car.

To get software updates for the AI system, there is an on-board electronic communication capability known as OTA (Over-The-Air). The OTA is also used to take the collected data from the on-board sensors and push it up into the cloud, allowing cloud-based servers to use the data to uncover additional Machine Learning and Deep Learning improvements about the driving task.

At some point, if the driverless car is an EV (Electrical Vehicle), it likely needs to be parked and plugged into a charger to get the electrical power pumped back up.

While the self-driving car is sitting there, presumably the AI has nothing much to do. The computers on-board the driverless car is relatively idle at that time.

Guess what, you could potentially use those idle computing cycles to search for intelligent life!

Yes, one means of leveraging the topnotch processors of a self-driving car would be to engage them in the same kind of radio signal processing that your home computer can do.

A downloaded and bona fide SETI program could be sitting in the memory of the self-driving car and be activated when the car is parked and doing nothing else of merit. Via OTA, radio signal data would be downloaded into the on-board computer memory, and once the analysis is done, the results could be pushed up into the cloud.

Might as well use the car's computers for something that can possibly help mankind.

You might be puzzled about the efficacy of having one self-driving car help in this manner, which doesn't seem like a moving-the-needle kind of assistance, so why bother with it.

There are about 250 million conventional cars in the United States today. Eventually, inexorably, it is assumed that those conventional cars will be retired and gradually be replaced by self-driving cars.

Some argue that we might not need the same number of driverless cars, meaning that we might end-up with some lesser number of driverless cars to provide the equivalent transport volume as today's 250 million conventional cars.

Meanwhile, an equally compelling argument is that we might end up with more driverless cars than the number of today's conventional cars, doing so because of the principle of induced demand. Induced demand is the concept that once you start something new it can bring forth added demand that was previously being suppressed.

If people that today are mobility disadvantaged opt to use driverless cars, and if we all become expectant of near-instantaneous mobility-on-demand, the number of driverless cars needed to fulfill societal needs could well exceed the number of today's conventional cars.

Anyway, putting aside this unresolved debate about the count, perhaps we can all agree that there is likely to be at least some hundred if not many hundreds of millions of driverless cars in our future.

If all those millions upon millions of self-driving cars were using their top-end computers to analyze the radio signals, it would be a huge boost in the search effort.

It could be a game-changer in the search for intelligent life.

Fleet owners of driverless cars could establish a SETI search capability into their fleet. As a passenger, you might be utterly clueless that the fleet is supporting the intelligent life search effort.

Or, the automaker or fleet owner might intentionally want you to know about the search activities, using their largesse as a kind of marketing ploy.

Hey, you all, use our ridesharing driverless cars since you are then supporting the search for intelligent life.

I've so far emphasized that the on-board computers would be only leveraged when the driverless car is parked and has no other task at hand, but this is not the only circumstance that could allow for doing the radio signal analyses.

As a human driver, you know that there are times while driving a car that involves sitting still and idling, such as when you are waiting at a red light or waiting to make a right turn and there is a pedestrian crossing in the crosswalk.

During those idle moments, the on-board computer could spare a few cycles and crunch further on the radio signal data.

Computers operate at tremendously fast speeds, and thus a handful of seconds that to you or me doesn't seem like much available time is a ton of computational time for the on-board processors.

We can up the ante.

Your driverless car is on the freeway and zooming along. There is no other significant traffic nearby. The driving scene is pretty much barren of anything other than simply driving in a straight line.

Yes, the on-board computers could potentially do some alien outer space life searching during those moments too.

Conclusion

Two birds with one stone.

You can have driverless cars and meanwhile also be improving the search efforts to discover intelligent life on other planets.

It seems like a great combo deal.

Not so fast!

There are some potential drawbacks.

First, some might argue that any "spare" moments of the on-board computers ought to go toward the number one priority of driving the car.

Even though a car is sitting at a red light, there is still the opportunity to be continually examining and re-examining the driving scene. The case can be made that the computers in a self-driving car should be exclusively used toward the driving task, at all times, including when the driverless car is parked (it could be reviewing it's driving efforts of the day and finding improvements in how to drive better).

As such, you can put your foot down and declare that the computers are sacrosanct on a self-driving car and must be solely devoted to being able to drive.

Another concern is that the program used to search for intelligent life might somehow go awry.

Suppose the search software causes the on-board computers to get into a locked-up loop and those computers are unable to be switched over into the driving mode. Not a good outcome.

Indeed, the classic line of "first, do no harm" is a crucial one for anything that is running on-board the computers inside the driverless car.

Worse too, suppose someone attaches a computer virus to the search program.

A fleet owner that has downloaded the search software is providing a goldmine form of access to the virus maker. In a trojan horse manner, the nefarious virus could be easily and readily pushed out to millions of driverless cars, doing so under the innocent guise of trying to help mankind.

You can see why there are some that eschews the idea of using driverless cars to aid in the intelligent life search.

No sense in taking any chances with a multi-ton automobile that somehow could go astray, all due to a "silly" and unlikely chance of detecting creatures in outer space.

On the other hand, there are those that hate to see computing cycles go to waste and perceive the advent of self-driving cars as a boon to the number of topnotch computers that we will have on this planet.

Should all those computers be doing nothing of consequence when they have idle time?

Can't we put in place enough safeguards to ensure that the search for intelligent life by self-driving cars is intelligently and safely devised?

Right now, the automakers and tech firms are struggling with just trying to get self-driving cars to drive properly, let alone be worried about the search for intelligent life.

You likely won't see anyone seriously entertaining this topic for years to come, only once the advent of true self-driving cars seems more assured.

One final thought.

Suppose though that the sooner we could find intelligent life, the sooner we might learn of tech advances that we haven't yet conceived of. Perhaps the delay in using self-driving cars for finding intelligent life might delay our discovering that we can beam humans like in Star Trek and dispense with cars of any kind.

Oops, that's not necessarily a good business model for the automakers.

CHAPTER 3
PIZZA DELIVERIES MYSTERY
AND
AI SELF-DRIVING CARS

CHAPTER 3

PIZZA DELIVERIES MYSTERY
AND
AI SELF-DRIVING CARS

A recent news report indicates that a man has been receiving pizza deliveries for nearly a decade.

That might not seem like earth-shattering news, except for the fact that the pizzas were not ordered by the man and he says that he has no idea why the pizzas are coming to him.

Now that's a mouthful.

And a stumper.

At first, he apparently relished those free pizzas and was not especially bothered by the underlying mystery of why they were being sent to him. He initially was dutifully concerned that the wrong address was being used, or that the pizzas were being delivered to the wrong house and therefore attempted to rebuff the deliveries.

But it seems that the pizzas were indeed aiming to arrive at his doorstep.

After a while, the matter became more of an irritant and an unwelcome guest.

Proof, perhaps, that even the allure and attraction of mouthwatering pizza can be at times too much of a good thing.

In fact, he indicates that when he gets wind of a pizza heading to his home, he begins to tense up and actually dreads the arrival.

One could certainly understand his angst and imagine that something like this could cause you to have heartburn when even thinking about pizza, no matter how sizzling it is and despite being topped with all the works.

He is baffled by the very notion that someone has opted to send him these unwanted and unordered pizzas.

Sure, it could happen maybe once or twice, yet to continue to take place over many years is eerie.

Is there some dastardly evildoer that believes that free pizza deliveries for life are a means to ruin another person's existence?

Could a ghost of a prior pizza life be playing haunting tricks on him?

Or, maybe he irked someone that figured the best revenge was to be served on a hot plate (or, is that supposed to be a cold plate) and came up with a crazy vengeance tactic of sending him pizzas?

If we put on our Sherlock Holmes cap, or perhaps more applicably Inspector Clouseau's trench coat, one has to ask relatively straightforward questions that would presumably clear-up this anchovy filled conundrum.

Who is paying for those pizza deliveries?

One would assume that if you follow the money, the trail has got to inevitably lead to the culprit that has the pizza retribution cahoots going on.

There might be two ways in which money is entering into the picture, namely via paying for the pizza maker to make the pizzas and/or via paying the pizza deliverer to deliver the pizzas.

It could be that the pizza maker takes the order and will automatically arrange for the delivery, thus, the money only shows-up upon the act of ordering the pizzas. Or, it could be that the pizza maker gets the dough for making the pizza (yes, that was an intended pun), and a separate delivery service is used and as a result, the second handover of money happens.

In either case, knowing who is paying for this charade would seem to get this mystery one step closer to being solved.

Plus, maybe there's a bizarre twist, which always seems to happen in detective stories and in the midst of solving a great mystery, which is maybe the butler did it, or in this case, perhaps the man receiving the pizzas is secretly sending the pizzas to himself, all as part of a plot to create a buzz.

If that twist doesn't seem palatable, suppose he has a beloved pet dog that has been ordering the pizzas, either for the dog to eat (be careful, do not let your dog eat pizza unwatched and unmanaged since pizza ingredients can be harmful to the pooch) or maybe as a loving tribute to his adored human owner.

Endless possibilities abound.

Apparently, the mystery includes that the pizzas do not always come from the same pizza maker and nor via the same pizza delivery service. That does make things a bit more challenging in terms of trying to stop the onslaught since otherwise, you could just tell the one pizza maker or the mainstay pizza delivery service to cease and desist their actions.

Of course, the problem with that spurning option is that if the man ever really wanted to get a pizza, it would require some quite hearty convincing with the pizza maker and pizza deliverer, presumably they would be highly resistant to any pizza orders culminating in his address.

Though this seems a worthwhile tradeoff in the battle to halt the endless procession of unwanted pizzas.

I'm sure that you might be thinking that he should give up trying to thwart the arrival of the pizzas and possibly do something else with the pizzas that he doesn't wish to himself consume.

Maybe start donating the pizzas to a charity.

Another idea would be to find out who else in his neighborhood likes pizza, and once those steaming pies arrive at his place, he could do a quick look-up on a list of which neighbor is next in line to get one. Just call them up and tell them their pizza has arrived, and voila, he would seemingly become the hero of his community (becoming acclaimed as the pizza man, because he can).

One downside for those getting these freebies is that they might get a pizza with toppings that they do not favor, possibly getting ones with tears generating onions or stomach-churning spicy sausage.

Currently, the pizzas are being delivered by human deliverers, but perhaps in the future, the deliveries will be via non-human hands.

How so?

We will gradually and inextricably be experiencing self-driving cars making deliveries to our homes, including for pizzas, plus food of all kinds, and for things like everyday groceries from the local store, and just about anything else that can reasonably be home-delivered.

This brings up today's interesting question: *Could AI-based true self-driving cars end-up delivering to someone's house an order even if the person had nothing to do with the order?*

Let's unpack the matter and see.

First, it will be useful to clarify what it means to refer to AI-based true self-driving cars.

The Role of AI-Based Self-Driving Cars

True self-driving cars are ones that the AI drives the car entirely on its own and there isn't any human assistance during the driving task.

These driverless vehicles are considered a Level 4 and Level 5, while a car that requires a human driver to co-share the driving effort is usually considered at a Level 2 or Level 3. The cars that co-share the driving task are described as being semi-autonomous, and typically contain a variety of automated add-on's that are referred to as ADAS (Advanced Driver-Assistance Systems).

There is not yet a true self-driving car at Level 5, which we don't yet even know if this will be possible to achieve, and nor how long it will take to get there.

Meanwhile, the Level 4 efforts are gradually trying to get some traction by undergoing very narrow and selective public roadway trials, though there is controversy over whether this testing should be allowed per se (we are all life-or-death guinea pigs in an experiment taking place on our highways and byways, some point out).

Since semi-autonomous cars require a human driver, the adoption of those types of cars won't be markedly different than driving conventional vehicles, so there's not much new per se to cover about them on this topic (though, as you'll see in a moment, the points next made are generally applicable). For semi-autonomous cars, it is important that the public needs to be forewarned about a disturbing aspect that's been arising lately, namely that in spite of those human drivers that keep posting videos of themselves falling asleep at the wheel of a Level 2 or Level 3 car, we all need to avoid being misled into believing that the driver can take away their attention from the driving task while driving a semi-autonomous car.

You are the responsible party for the driving actions of the vehicle, regardless of how much automation might be tossed into a Level 2 or Level 3.

Self-Driving Cars And Home Deliveries

For Level 4 and Level 5 true self-driving vehicles, there won't be a human driver involved in the driving task.

All occupants will be passengers.

The AI is doing the driving.

Pundits anticipate that the use of true self-driving cars will further spur the ongoing home-delivery spark that has already grabbed hold in recent times.

Why so?

The use of self-driving cars is predicted to lower the cost of home delivery, partially due to excising the labor cost involved in hiring a human driver, and thus spike or fuel (one might say) home delivery efforts.

There is one looming problem, which deals with the so-called "last mile" problem or more likely the final fifty feet or so.

When a self-driving car arrives to deliver you something, right now the vehicle pulls up to the curb and you need to come out to get the items being delivered. For those that prefer not to get things while wearing their pajamas, or for those that cannot physically readily go out to the curb, the last fifty feet is an unbearable barrier that for them is unfulfilled by a self-driving car.

Solutions to this issue are being crafted and tested.

For example, the self-driving car could be carrying a smaller self-driving vehicle that is launched from the self-driving car, and this mini-me rolls up to the door of the home. Another approach involves a crawling robot, typically a four-legged contraption, and it crawls out of the self-driving car and makes the final delivery.

There are also two-legged robots that look somewhat human-like in appearance, and those might get out of the self-driving car and walk up to your door.

Nobody yet knows whether the general public will be accepting of these robot-based delivery methods.

The little rolling robots are already doing pretty well as being generally accepted, perhaps because they seem harmless looking and remind us of the sci-fi portrayals of pleasing robots, while the robots that crawl or walk might seem scary or imposing, so we'll need to see if people will get used to those kinds of mechanical creatures among us.

Do not though assume that all home delivery will be bereft of a human deliverer.

It could be that the self-driving car has a human riding along, doing so to deal with that final fifty feet of getting any carried goods from the parked vehicle to the door of the consumer. Note that the human deliverer does not need to have a driver's license and has no involvement in the driving of the vehicle, which, as such, can possibly aid in reducing the cost of home delivery (somewhat) versus when the home deliverer is also the driver and needs to have a license to drive.

If the home delivery also includes assembling a piece of furniture or offering in-home value-added services, the odds then are that a human would in fact need to come along, either accompanying the delivery of the good itself or arriving at some other point in time.

In short, we ought to anticipate that home delivery is going to be amped by the advent of self-driving cars and that human hands might still be involved (though not for driving purposes).

Pizza Delivery Mystery If Self-Driving Cars Involved

We can now revisit the story of the mysterious pizza deliveries.

A self-driving car comes up to your domicile and proclaims to you that your pizza has arrived.

Could it ever be that the pizza is not intended for your place?

Sure, absolutely, there is certainly a possibility of a "mistaken" delivery.

Suppose the order when placed had stated the wrong address.

The AI driving system would obediently deliver the order to the incorrect address (incorrect as stated by the order) since the AI would not have any reason to believe that the address is somehow a mistake (unless the address was non-existent or had some other look-up problem as not a valid address).

Also, it could be that perhaps a buddy or the like has opted to wish you a happy birthday by sending you a pizza, unannounced, or maybe you have won the latest Reader's Digest sweepstakes and got a pizza delivered to your home, all of which intentionally specified your address, and the AI delivered to where it was informed to do so.

My point is that for those that somehow believe AI will be all-knowing, put that notion aside, and realize that the AI will likely take the same kinds of actions that any human driver and pizza deliverer would aim to do, consisting of dutifully delivering that pizza to the stated address.

As an aside, some believe that AI will ultimately become sentient, arriving in a moment characterized as the singularity and that this sentience will be a form of full or complete AI, sometimes referred to as having Artificial General Intelligence (AGI), and Artificial Super Intelligence (ASI) for superhuman AGI.

Would a sentient AI that perhaps has evolved into ASI be a pizza deliverer?

It seems a bit less fulfilling as a suitable use of such intelligence, but, hey, everyone and presumably everything has to make a living.

Anyway, we have established that the AI-based true self-driving car could deliver pizzas to someone that did not necessarily order the pies.

Would we be able to use our Sherlock and Clouseau gumshoe skills to figure out who sent the pizzas?

In essence, we seemingly should be able to identify who placed the order with the pizza maker and/or with the self-driving car service that delivered the pizza.

One supposes so, though it could be further wrapped in a cloak, such as if the purchaser was using a Bitcoin-like cryptocurrency and perhaps overtly attempting to hide their identity.

A small twist in this too is that there are some pizza makers that will no longer be making pizzas by human hands and instead be made by a robot.

Plus, there are even some indications that a self-driving vehicle might embody the pizza-making capability and thus double as both pizza maker and pizza delivery platform.

Two for the price of one.

If timed properly by the AI driving system, the pizza could be cooking while on the way to your home, arriving just as the freshly-baked pizza reaches its peak of culinary perfection, rather than having sat around in a stuffy cardboard box during the journey to your place.

In terms of the unwanted pizza deliveries, perhaps with a self-driving car that at least the AI could alert the intended receiver of the pizza that the pie is on its way, making use of V2X technology (there will be V2V for vehicle-to-vehicle electronic communications, and V2P for vehicle-to-pedestrian, along with other targeted communiques which are generally referred to as the "X" in V2X). In that case, the receiver might be able to prevent the delivery by responding accordingly to the V2X communications.

Also, it is anticipated that self-driving cars might likely be owned in large fleets, whereby a big company such as a major automaker or a rental car firm or a ride-sharing business would own massive sized fleets of self-driving cars. In that case, the person that is getting the uninvited pizzas could contact the fleet owner and ask that the entire fleet be warned to not bring pizzas to a particular address.

Where there is a will, there is a way.

Conclusion

You can easily envision that if a self-driving car was involved in delivering these mystery pizzas, it would have generated worldwide headlines, including the press clamoring to the rooftops that an AI system has gone berserk and mindlessly and robotically is delivering unsolicited pizzas.

Nope, right now, it is in the hands of humans.

Everyday, normal, like you and me, humans.

A lesson to be learned from this otherwise unorthodox matter of the pizza deliveries is that when replacing a human-performed task with an AI-performed task, we cannot assume that the AI will necessarily do a "better" job, and nor can we assume that the AI will do a lesser or worse job.

I bring this up because we are rapidly heading toward a tsunami of AI systems that will surround and be involved in most things that we do.

When things happen to go awry, the likely first finger pointing will be at the AI.

I'm not suggesting that the AI will be innocent in the matter, and in fact, I have repeatedly exhorted that we need to be on our guard that AI systems are not as yet able to embody common sense and we ought to not anthropomorphize them, yet we also should not ascribe faults to AI that are potentially unmerited or misdirected.

Say, that brings up a curious final point, do you think there's a chance that an AI system is the one sending all of those pizzas to that man that doesn't want them?

Perhaps the AI is toying with us, already on the verge of super-intelligence, and figured that it would subtly show its AI mastermind hand, as it were, by repeatedly sending unsought pizzas.

Are we smart enough to make sense of the breadcrumb clues that the AI is leaving for us?

Think carefully about this, especially the next time you consume a thoughtful slice of a savory baked pizza.

CHAPTER 4

PROVABLY BENEFICIAL AI
AND
AI SELF-DRIVING CARS

Dr. Lance B. Eliot

CHAPTER 4

PROVABLY BENEFICIAL AI

AND

AI SELF-DRIVING CARS

AI systems are being crafted and fielded at lightning-like speeds.

That seems on the surface to be a good thing.

But do we know that these AI systems are going to act in beneficial ways?

Perhaps among the plethora of AI systems are some that will be or might become untoward, working in non-beneficial ways, carrying out detrimental acts that in some manner cause irreparable harm, injury, and possibly even death to humans.

Yes, there is a distinct possibility that there are toxic AI systems among the ones that are aiming to help mankind.

In fact, we really do not know whether it might be just a scant few that are reprehensible or whether it might be the preponderance that goes that malevolent route.

One crucial twist that accompanies an AI system is that they are often devised to learn while in use, thus, there is a real chance that the original intent will be waylaid and overtaken into foul territory, doing so over time, and ultimately exceed any preset guardrails and veer into evil-doing.

Proponents of AI cannot assume that AI will necessarily always be cast toward goodness.

There is the noble desire to achieve *AI For Good*, and likewise the ghastly underbelly of *AI For Bad*.

To clarify, even if AI developers had something virtuous in mind, realize that their creation can either on its own transgress into badness as it adjusts on-the-fly via Machine Learning (ML) and Deep Learning (DL), or it could contain unintentionally seeded errors or omissions that when later encountered during use are inadvertently going to generate bad acts.

Somebody ought to be doing something about this, you might be thinking and likewise wringing your hands worryingly.

One such proposed solution is an arising focus on *provably beneficial AI*.

Here's the background.

If an AI system could be mathematically modeled, it might be feasible to perform a mathematical proof that would logically indicate whether the AI will be beneficial or not.

As such, anyone embarking on putting an AI system into the world would be able to run the AI through this provability approach and then be confident that their AI will clearly be in the *AI For Good* camp, and those that endeavor to use the AI or that become reliant upon the AI will be comforted by the aspect that the AI was proven to be beneficial.

Voila, we turn the classic notion of A is to B, and as B is to C, into the strongly logical conclusion that A is to C, as a kind of tightly interwoven mathematical logic that can be applied to AI.

For those that look to the future and see a potential for AI that might overtake mankind, perhaps becoming a futuristic version of a frightening Frankenstein, this idea of clamping down on AI by having it undergo a provability mechanism to ensure it is beneficial offers much relief and excitement.

We all ought to rejoice in the goal of being able to provably showcase that an AI system is beneficial.

Well, other than those that are on the foul side of AI, aiming to use AI for devious deeds and purposely seeking to do *AI For Bad*. They would be likely to eschew any such proofs and offer instead pretenses perhaps that their AI is aimed at goodness as a means of distracting from its true goals (meanwhile, some might come straight out and proudly proclaim they are making AI for destructive aspirations, the so-called Dr. Evil flair).

There seems to be little doubt that overall, the world would be better off if there was such a thing as provably beneficial AI.

We could use it on AI that is being unleashed into the real-world and then is heartened that we have done our best to keep AI from doing us in, and accordingly use our remaining energies on keeping watch on the non-proven AI that is either potentially afoul or that might be purposely crafted to be adverse.

Regrettably, there is a rub.

The rub is that wanting to have a means for creating or verifying provably beneficial AI is a lot harder than it might sound.

Let's consider one such approach.

Professor Stuart Russell at the University of California Berkeley is at the forefront of provably beneficial AI and offers in his research that there are three core principles involved:

1) "The machine's purpose is to maximize the realization of human values. In particular, it has no purposes of its own and no innate desire to protect itself."

2) "The machine is initially uncertain about what those human values are. The machine may learn more about human values as it goes along, of course, but it may never achieve complete certainty."

3) "Machines can learn about human values by overserving the choices that we humans make."

Those core principles are then formulated into a mathematical framework, and an AI system is either designed and built according to those principles from the ground-up, or an existent AI system might be retrofitted to abide by those principles (the retrofitting would be generally unwise as it is easier and more parsimonious to start things the right way rather than trying to, later on, squeeze a square peg into a round hole, as it were).

For those of you that are AI insiders, you might recognize this approach as being characterized by being a Cooperative Inverse Reinforcement Learning (CIRL) scheme, whereby multiple agents are working in a cooperative manner and the agents, in this case, are a human and an AI, of which the AI attempts to learn from the human by the actions of the human instead of learning from the AI's own direct actions per se.

Setting aside the technical jargon, some would bluntly say that this particular approach to provably beneficial AI is shaped around making humans happy with the results of the AI efforts.

And making humans happy sure seems like a laudable ambition.

The Complications Involved

It turns out that there is no free lunch in trying to achieve provably beneficial AI.

Consider some of the core principles and what they bring about.

The first stated principle is that the AI is aimed to maximize the realization of human values and that the AI has no purposes of its own, including no desire to protect itself.

Part of the basis for making this rule is that it would seem to do away with the classic paperclip problem or the King Midas problem of AI.

Allow me to explain.

Hypothetically, suppose an AI system was set up to produce paperclips. If the AI is solely devoted to that function, it might opt to do so in ways that are detrimental to mankind. For example, in an effort to produce as many paperclips as possible, the AI begins to takeover steel production to ensure that there are sufficient materials to make paperclips. Soon, in a draconian way, the AI has marshaled all of the world's resources to incessantly make those darned paperclips.

Plus, horrifically, humanity might be deemed as getting in the way of the paperclip production, and so the AI then wipes out humanity too.

All in all, this is decidedly not what we would have hoped for as a result of the AI paperclip making system.

This is similar to the fable of King Midas whereby everything he touched turned to gold, which at first seemed like a handy way to great rich, but then upon touching water it turns to gold, and the food turned to gold, and so on, ultimately he does himself in and realizes that his wishes were a curse.

Thus, rather than AI having a goal that it embodies, such as making paperclips, the belief in this version of provably beneficial AI is that it would be preferred that the AI not have any self-beliefs and instead entirely be driven by the humans around it.

Notice too that the principle states that the AI is established such that it has no desire to protect itself.

Why so?

Aha, this relates to another classic AI problem, the off-switch or kill-switch issue.

Assume that any AI that we humans craft will have some form of off-switch or kill-switch, meaning that if we wanted to do so, we could stop the AI, presumably whenever we deemed desirable to so halt. Certainly, this would be a smart thing for us to do, else we might have that crazed paperclip maker and have no means to prevent it from overwhelming the planet in paperclips.

If the AI has any wits about it, which we are kind of assuming it would, the AI would be astute enough to realize that there is an off-switch and that humans could use it. But if the AI is doggedly determined to make those paperclips, the use of an off-switch would prevent it from meeting its overarching goal, and therefore the proper thing to do would be for the AI to disable that kill-switch.

In fact, it might be one of the first and foremost acts that the AI would undertake, seeking to preserve its own "lifeblood" by disabling the off switch.

To try and get around this potential loophole, the stated principle in this provably beneficial AI framework indicates that the AI is not going to have that kind of self-preservation cooked into its inherent logic.

Presumably, if the AI is going to seek to maximize the realization of human values, it could be that the AI will itself realize that disabling the off-switch is not in keeping with the needs of society and thus will refrain from doing so. Furthermore, maybe the AI eventually realizes that it cannot achieve the realization of human values, or that it has begun to violate that key premise, and the AI might overtly turn itself off, viewing that its own "demise" is the best way to accede to human values.

This does seem enterprising and perhaps gets us out of the AI doomsday predicaments.

Not everyone sees it that way.

One concern is that if the AI does not have a cornerstone of any semblance of self, it will potentially be readily swayed in directions that are not quite so desirable for humanity.

Essentially, without a truism at its deepest realm of something ironclad about don't harm humans, using perhaps Issac Asimov's famous first rule that a robot may not injure a human being or via inaction allow a human to be harmed, there is no failsafe of preventing the AI from going kilter.

That being said, the counter-argument is that the core principles of this kind of provably beneficial AI are indicative that the AI will learn about human values, doing so by observation of human acts, and we might assume this includes that the AI will inevitably and inextricably discover on its own Asimov's first rule, doing so by the mere act of observing human behavior.

Will it?

A counter to the counter-argument is that the AI might learn that humans do kill each other, somewhat routinely and with at times seemingly little regard for human life, out of which the AI might then divine that it is okay to harm or kill humans.

Since the AI lacks any ingrained precept that precludes harming humans, the AI will be open to whatever it seems to "learn" about humans, including the worst and exceedingly vile of acts.

Additionally, those that are critics of this variant of provably beneficial AI that are apt to point out that the word "beneficial" is potentially being used in a misleading and confounding way.

It would seem that the core principles do not mean to achieve "beneficial" in that sense of arriving at a decidedly "good" result per se (in any concrete or absolute way), and instead beneficial is intended as relative to whatever humans happen to be exhibiting as seemingly so-called beneficial behavior. This might be construed as relativistic ethics stanch, and in that manner, does not abide by any presumed everlasting or considered unequivocal rules of how humans ought to behave (even if they do not necessarily behave in such ways).

You can likely see that this topic can indubitably get immersed in and possibly mired into cornerstone philosophical and ethical foundations debates.

This also takes things into the qualms about basing the AI on the behaviors of humans.

We all know that oftentimes humans say one thing and yet do another.

As such, one might construe that it is best to base the AI on what people do, rather than what they say since their actions presumably speak louder than their words. The problem with this viewpoint of humanity is that it seems to omit that words do matter and that inspection of behavior alone might be a rather narrow means of ascribing things like intent, which would seem to be an equally important element for consideration.

There is also the open question about which humans are to be observed.

Suppose the humans are part of a cult that is bent on death and destruction, and in which case, their "happiness" might be shaped around the beliefs that lead to those dastardly results, and the AI would apparently dutifully "learn" those as the thing to maximize as human values.

And so on.

In short, as pointed out earlier, seeking to devise an approach for provably beneficial AI is a lot more challenging than meets the eye at first glance.

That being said, we should not cast aside the goal of finding a means to arrive at provably beneficial AI.

Keep on trucking, as they say.

Meanwhile, how might the concepts of provably beneficial AI be applied in a real-world context?

Consider the matter of AI-based true self-driving cars.

The Role of AI-Based Self-Driving Cars

True self-driving cars are ones that the AI drives the car entirely on its own and there isn't any human assistance during the driving task.

These driverless vehicles are considered a Level 4 and Level 5, while a car that requires a human driver to co-share the driving effort is usually considered at a Level 2 or Level 3. The cars that co-share the driving task are described as being semi-autonomous, and typically contain a variety of automated add-on's that are referred to as ADAS (Advanced Driver-Assistance Systems).

There is not yet a true self-driving car at Level 5, which we don't yet even know if this will be possible to achieve, and nor how long it will take to get there.

Meanwhile, the Level 4 efforts are gradually trying to get some traction by undergoing very narrow and selective public roadway trials, though there is controversy over whether this testing should be allowed per se (we are all life-or-death guinea pigs in an experiment taking place on our highways and byways, some point out).

Since semi-autonomous cars require a human driver, the adoption of those types of cars won't be markedly different than driving conventional vehicles, so there's not much new per se to cover about them on this topic (though, as you'll see in a moment, the points next made are generally applicable).

For semi-autonomous cars, it is important that the public needs to be forewarned about a disturbing aspect that's been arising lately, namely that in spite of those human drivers that keep posting videos of themselves falling asleep at the wheel of a Level 2 or Level 3 car, we all need to avoid being misled into believing that the driver can take away their attention from the driving task while driving a semi-autonomous car.

You are the responsible party for the driving actions of the vehicle, regardless of how much automation might be tossed into a Level 2 or Level 3.

Self-Driving Cars And Home Deliveries

For Level 4 and Level 5 true self-driving vehicles, there won't be a human driver involved in the driving task.

All occupants will be passengers.

The AI is doing the driving.

One hope for true self-driving cars is that they will mitigate the approximate 40,000 deaths and about 1.2 million annual injuries that occur due to human driving in the United States alone each year. The assumption is that since the AI won't be driving and drinking, for example, it will not incur drunk driving-related car crashes (which accounts for nearly a third of all driving fatalities).

Some offer the following "absurdity" instance for those that are considering the notion of provably beneficial AI as an approach based on observing human behavior.

Suppose AI observes the existing driving practices of humans. Undoubtedly, it will witness that humans crash into other cars, and presumably not know that it is due to being intoxicated (in that one-third or so of such instances).

Presumably, we as humans allow those humans to do that kind of driving and cause those kinds of deaths.

We must, therefore, be "satisfied" with the result, else why we would allow it to continue.

The AI then "learns" that it is okay to ram and kill other humans in such car crashes, and has no semblance that it is due to drinking and that it is an undesirable act that humans would prefer to not have taken place.

Would the AI be able to discern that this is not something it should be doing?

I realize that those of you in the provably beneficial AI camp will be chagrined at this kind of characterization, and indeed there are loopholes in the aforementioned logic, but the point generally is that these are quite complex matters and undoubtedly disconcerting in many ways.

Even the notion of having foundational precepts as absolutes is not so readily viable either.

Take as a quick example the assertion by some that an AI driving system ought to have an absolute rule like Asimov's about not harming humans and thus this apparently resolves any possible misunderstanding or mushiness on the topic.

But, as I've pointed out in an analysis of a recent incident in which a man rammed his car into an active shooter, there are going to be circumstances whereby we might want an AI driving system to undertake harm, and cannot necessarily have one ironclad rule thereof.

Again, there is no free lunch, in any direction, that one takes on these matters.

Conclusion

There is really no question that we could greatly benefit from a viable means to provably showcase that AI is beneficial.

If we cannot attain showing that the AI is beneficial, at least provide a mathematical proof that the AI will keep to its stated requirements (well, this opens another can of worms, but at least sidesteps the notion of "beneficial," rightfully or wrongly so).

Imagine an AI-based self-driving car that was subjected before getting onto the roadways to a provable safety theorem, and that had something similar that worked in real-time as the vehicle navigated our public streets.

There are researchers trying to get there and we can all hope they keep trying.

At this juncture, one thing that is provably the case is that all of the upcoming AI that is rapidly emerging into society is going to be extraordinarily vexing and troublesome, and that's something we can easily prove.

CHAPTER 5
CITY STREETS PAINTINGS
AND
AI SELF-DRIVING CARS

CHAPTER 5
CITY STREETS PAINTINGS AND AI SELF-DRIVING CARS

If you follow the news, you most likely have seen the recent efforts of numerous cities that have painted large block letters onto their streets.

In many cases, the streets are considered active in that once the painting has been completed, the roadway is reopened to everyday traffic. Thus, these are not seemingly specially set aside streets that are secured from vehicular traversal and instead are put back into their usual service after having been painted.

Customarily, paint that is used on an active traffic-going street is employed as a traffic control device, known in the roadway infrastructure realm as "road surface markings" and are used to officially depict navigational guidelines and directions.

When drivers proceed along a street, they are at times provided visual cues via painted asphalt surfaces that showcase where the median is, where crosswalks are, and generally is indicative of the curbs and other key roadway features. The colors of yellow and of white are particularly reserved for these purposes and drivers are accustomed to noting where those painted lines and areas are.

A driver that is familiar with a given street is apt to no longer overtly notice the painted surfaces, though they seemingly subconsciously still pay attention to the guidance and use it reflexively as they drive down a street so marked.

Drivers that have not previously entered onto a particular street and are approaching it for the first time are likely to be directly cognizant of the painted guidance, using it actively as they attempt to safely make their way along that street.

Federal standards for the use of painted surfaces as a traffic control device are included in a governmentally approved document referred to as the MUTCD (Manual on Uniform Traffic Control Devices for Streets and Highways) as published by the Federal Highway Administration (FHWA) and the Office of Transportation Operations (HOTO).

Additionally, the FHWA issued an official ruling on the various uses of painted surfaces as a supplemental memorandum.

Part of the reason that a supplement memorandum was produced involved a rising interest by cities in painting murals and other artistic renderings onto active streets and in-use roadway surfaces.

Why is painted art on the roadway worthy of added consideration and potential concern?

Some have expressed qualms that the artistry displayed could be distracting to those driving on such streets.

A driver might mistakenly interpret a portion of the artistic rendering to be a driving guidance directive and therefore drive improperly, either illegally driving or potentially driving in a means that could endanger themselves and other nearby drivers, perhaps also jeopardizing pedestrians.

Or, a driver might become distracted by the artistic presentation and thus fail to realize that a car ahead of them is braking suddenly, or that a pedestrian is jaywalking in front of the car.

As such, the driver might plow into another vehicle or ram into a pedestrian as a result of being focused on the art and bereft of attention to the driving situation.

Another possibility is that the painted art has overlapped, obscured, or confounded the intended painted traffic control surfaces.

Suppose that an artistic mural extends over a crosswalk and as a result, the formal crosswalk-painted lines are less identifiable or possibly even no longer discernable at all.

Thus, the paint markings intended for traffic safety are no longer viably able to be seen and the drivers of the roadway cannot as readily gauge the nature of how to best navigate the street.

The use of painted surfaces as a traffic control mechanism is supposed to be a visual indicator for drivers and something that is observed and abided by on nearly an instinctive basis while driving. Indeed, the use of nationwide standards has provided a uniformity that enables drivers to minimize uncertainty about what the paint is trying to tell them, becoming second nature in detection, and decidedly is not supposed to distract drivers from the life-or-death nature of the driving task (i.e., the painted surfaces are considered a crucial aid to the driving task and the safety thereof).

So, when there is paint used on an active roadway surface and that paint does not have an ascertained traffic guidance purpose, one logical question arises as to whether the painted conveyance will undercut traffic safety or whether it will be neutral or, surprisingly to some, possibly even bolster traffic safety.

Let's take a look at the potential outcomes.

Art murals are usually an aesthetic treatment, generally done for artistry purposes, and not as a goal of aiding traffic per se.

Likewise, it would seem that the use of large block letters is not usually being undertaken as a traffic control means.

Some argue that any such painting that is not intended for bearing on roadway traversal or street navigation is usurping safety and will ultimately generate added traffic injuries and fatalities.

Obviously, if so, this would be an adverse unintended consequence.

In that frame of reference, what tradeoff is to be used when weighing the value of the painted surface that is not for roadway navigation versus not putting such painted artistry or messages onto the given street being otherwise used for designated driving purposes?

Even formally added painted conventions for roadway control tend to undergo scrutiny.

For example, recent extensions of the roadway painting approach for driving purposes have included the adoption of green painted lanes and street markings to designate bicycle riding zones. This is being done to encourage bike riding and hopefully guide car drivers to be cautious and aware of nearby bicyclists. Nonetheless, studies have been undertaken about the impacts on driving safety and whether the green painted markings are worthwhile or not.

When other non-driving painted efforts opt to use paint that is yellow, white, or green, do those color choices possibly make differentiating the actual roadway surfaces even harder for drivers?

Do drivers potentially become numb to any painted markings if the use of paint on the roadway surfaces is undertaken for all sorts of purposes?

Note that this kind of painting is also a potential complication for pedestrians. Pedestrians might assume that a painted area that seems to have a message or artistry is reserved for access by pedestrians and thusly wander into the street to more closely examine the painted surface. Those pedestrians might become distracted as they perhaps take pictures or look directly at the ground, meanwhile failing to be observant of cars that might be coming down the street.

Furthermore, pedestrians coming upon such a street are perhaps apt to enter into the street and disrupt traffic, causing driver delays, which some assert can foster road rage or other untoward driving acts.

Those with a penchant for eschewing the use of paint for anything but roadway control are prone to arguing that the streets should first get a makeover of the potholes and cracks, for which the added paint can at times hide. This hiding factor means too that drivers might fail to avoid those roadway imperfections, damaging their cars or causing them to drive awry, and too that the now concealed nature of the potholes and cracks will diminish the odds of infrastructure improvements to remove or fix those roadway blemishes.

It might seem at first glance that the stance of painting non-control exhibitory displays is fraught with so many downsides that it ought not to be undertaken altogether.

There is another side to this coin.

Some point out that there are potentially traffic-calming effects that can bolster safety on those streets.

Presumably, drivers will slow down due to the extra painted surfaces, either due to lack of familiarity and wanting to figure out how to navigate the street or due to being interested in whatever the added painted aspects are seeking to convey.

Coupled with this slowing down is the possibility that the drivers will be triggered to be more alert than normal.

Whereas they might have simply zoomed along and not given any direct attention to the street and any nearby pedestrians, the special nature of the additional markings has jolted them out of their usual driving stupor. Research studies that have examined these types of matters are often difficult to compare as to conclusive findings due to the variability in such facets as the extent of the painted surfaces, the pre and post traffic patterns in existence on any given street, the temporary timeframe versus permanent application of the painted surfaces, and so on.

Lawsuits brought to contend with the added painted efforts can at times get mired in the jurisdictional boundaries involved, such as whether a particular street is under the guise of the local authorities or the state or federal jurisdiction.

One thing that can be seemingly inarguably said is that the painting of streets beyond the conventional roadway markings will undoubtedly continue for some time to come.

This brings up an interesting question: *Will AI-based true self-driving cars be able to cope with painted roadway surfaces that are beyond the scope of conventional roadway markings?*

Let's unpack the matter and see.

The Role of AI-Based Self-Driving Cars

True self-driving cars are ones that the AI drives the car entirely on its own and there isn't any human assistance during the driving task.

These driverless vehicles are considered a Level 4 and Level 5, while a car that requires a human driver to co-share the driving effort is usually considered at a Level 2 or Level 3. The cars that co-share the driving task are described as being semi-autonomous, and typically contain a variety of automated add-on's that are referred to as ADAS (Advanced Driver-Assistance Systems).

There is not yet a true self-driving car at Level 5, which we don't yet even know if this will be possible to achieve, and nor how long it will take to get there.

Meanwhile, the Level 4 efforts are gradually trying to get some traction by undergoing very narrow and selective public roadway trials, though there is controversy over whether this testing should be allowed per se (we are all life-or-death guinea pigs in an experiment taking place on our highways and byways, some point out).

Since semi-autonomous cars require a human driver, the adoption of those types of cars won't be markedly different than driving conventional vehicles, so there's not much new per se to cover about them on this topic (though, as you'll see in a moment, the points next made are generally applicable).

For semi-autonomous cars, it is important that the public needs to be forewarned about a disturbing aspect that's been arising lately, namely that despite those human drivers that keep posting videos of themselves falling asleep at the wheel of a Level 2 or Level 3 car, we all need to avoid being misled into believing that the driver can take away their attention from the driving task while driving a semi-autonomous car.

You are the responsible party for the driving actions of the vehicle, regardless of how much automation might be tossed into a Level 2 or Level 3.

Self-Driving Cars And Painted Roadways

For Level 4 and Level 5 true self-driving vehicles, there won't be a human driver involved in the driving task.

All occupants will be passengers.

The AI is doing the driving.

To drive a car, the AI relies upon a slew of special sensors that are added to a vehicle, including various cameras, radar devices, LIDAR, ultrasonic, thermal imaging, etc. The sensors are used to collect an indication of the surroundings and then synthesized together in an approach called sensor fusion or sometimes referred to as MSDF (Multi-Sensor Data Fusion).

The automakers and self-driving tech firms are each opting to construct sensor fusion algorithms of their choosing, and likewise selecting hardware sensors of their choosing.

This in turn means that it is problematic to make overly broad statements about what any specific brand or model of self-driving car might be able to do or not do.

In any case, generally, most of the self-driving cars are programmed to detect the painted surfaces of the roadway.

In fact, especially during the earlier days of self-driving car development, the painted lines and other markings were particularly crucial, and some might argue they were overly relied upon. A frequently employed "trick" or technique has involved a "follow the line" algorithm by the AI system and can be a dangerously simplistic means of driving.

The concern about this kind of overreliance stems from the possibility that painted lines and markings can readily fade over time, thus, being excessively dependent on such painted aspects alone is worrisome and could lead to adverse results.

Also, often there are painted lines and markings that are allowed to be discontinued in use and new ones painted elsewhere instead, yet the older and no longer used painted indications are still visible and can be (undesirably) detected.

Human drivers can get tripped up on such matters too, though they tend to be experienced in realizing that faded lines are not to be strictly observed and that the stronger or newer painted surfaces are likely to be the ones of attention (though, this is not necessarily an easy differentiation for humans to discern either).

Okay, so the AI of self-driving cars usually is programmed to use the camera images to look for painted surfaces.

So what?

Well, based on those analyzed images, the AI then directs the driving controls of the car, choosing to steer, hit the gas, or use the brakes, partially as a result of attempting to interpret the painted surfaces.

Some advocates of self-driving cars have vigorously been pushing to have the national roadway infrastructure get newly painted, freshening up and correcting potentially improperly painted areas, along with including specialized paints that are more modern and readily detectable.

Roadway infrastructure bills and propositions are being asked to include such matters.

The point is that by making those changes, it could bolster the advent of self-driving cars, which in of themselves are proffered to provide numerous benefits for society, including reducing the annual driving injuries and fatalities, along with becoming a mobility-for-all capability.

There are some in the self-driving car arena that fervently contends that the paint is the paint, meaning that the AI ought to be able to cope with the same faded and muddled painted surfaces that human drivers do, thus, there is not a need per se to make such changes, though they would tend to energetically support those changes as something that would enhance both human driver safety and AI self-driving car usage at the same time.

Of course, the AI is generally crafted to assume that the painted surfaces are existent for purposes of traffic control and roadway navigation, just as humans are likewise trained and become familiar with the same uses of painted markings.

How well does the AI do when painted roadway surfaces diverge from the norm?

It depends.

First, please know that today's AI does not have any semblance of common-sense reasoning and nor is the AI of today anywhere near being sentient or having reached the so-called singularity.

This is important to keep in mind since the AI is not going to magically or miraculously divine that an artistic mural is indeed an artistic mural, and nor that large block letters are a message beyond the scope of traffic navigation.

Generally, the AI would likely attempt the usual visual processing analyses and if it could not discern the true traffic-intended painted surfaces, it would likely fall back on its other sensory devices as an added aid (not necessarily for figuring out the paint, but for figuring out the roadway structure and its shape and form).

One would hope that the AI has been crafted to assume that the cameras might be non-functioning or faltering, therefore the AI should have fallback postures already instilled. We all know that when in snowy conditions, for example, the street markings are likely to be obscured, and thus the AI if well-rounded would be prepared for circumstances of something like added paint that obscures the official roadway painted markings.

What seems to be a bit more challenging consists of the painted markings potentially being confounded with the official ones, in which case the AI could be misled into assuming it "knows" the street guidance and yet it is misinterpreting the painted surfaces (which, could happen to human drivers too).

Many of the self-driving cars are being pre-loaded with detailed maps of the cities that they are driving in, and for which this then can potentially help to contend with situations involving roadway over-painting and the like.

By-and-large the automakers and self-driving car firms are including in their initial public tryouts the use of a human driver onboard, also known as a safety or back-up driver, doing so as the self-driving car is repeatedly perusing back-and-forth in a city area, attempting to train the AI on the driving particulars on those streets and yet having a human driver for any just-in-case circumstances.

Suppose that after being so trained, the AI is allowed to drive a self-driving car and there is no human back-up driver included.

Any subsequent painted changes might be potentially internally realized by the AI, being able to rely upon the prior "learned" image processing of those same streets and thus not become disturbed or distracted by the latest art mural or messaging that has been painted on a street.

Naturally, this type of fallback has to be performed with caution since the AI cannot immediately necessarily attribute the newly painted surfaces as being done for artistry or messaging in contrast to a city having painted new traffic control markings.

Conclusion

We might reasonably assume that the AI if properly devised will be able to generally contend with the added painted markings on roadway surfaces.

There is an added twist though.

Since we are going to have a mixture of both human-driven cars and AI self-driving cars, likely for decades to come, if the human drivers are kilter over the painted surfaces and opt to drive recklessly or without proper attention, there is a heightened chance that the self-driving car could ram into such a vehicle or that a human-driven car might ram into a self-driving car.

In any case, one does wonder that if AI progresses sufficiently, will it one day be driving along and upon detecting a painted art mural or a painted block letters message be able to robustly "understand" what it is, and maybe engage the passengers in a thought-provoking dialogue about the meaning and substance of the painted roadway aspects?

Time will tell.

CHAPTER 6

COPS SHOOTING AT VEHICLES
AND
AI SELF-DRIVING CARS

CHAPTER 6

COPS SHOOTING AT VEHICLES
AND
AI SELF-DRIVING CARS

One of the most controversial policing topics that society wrestles with is whether law enforcement officers should be able to shoot at a moving vehicle.

Generally, three overarching opinions on the matter seem to have emerged on this weighty topic.

Some insist that such an act should never be permitted. As notable emphasis, that means that no matter what the circumstances might be, no police officer is to ever shoot at a moving vehicle, period, end of the story.

In somewhat of a contrast, others indicate that the act can be undertaken though only rarely, allowing that there would be extraordinary exceptions that merit such dire action.

And then some would state that such an act can be done in the performance of law enforcement duties, for which the officer will ultimately need to justify their actions, and that trying to stipulate a narrow prespecified range of when such action can be undertaken is improperly hampering the officer and putting their life at undue risk and potentially likewise putting other innocents at risk too.

In short, the three mainstay approaches might be described as:
a) Never allowed
b) Allowed rarely if ever
c) Allowed in due course as merited

For those in the "never allowed" perspective, they would typically argue that the moment that you accept the other two options to be considered, you are opening a Pandora's box. To them, this is a strictly binary question and the answer is either that shooting at a moving vehicle is allowed or it is banned outright.

Once you progress into the allowed viewpoints, the "never allowed" would tend to say that you are going to have a slew of instances and that some might be bona fide and yet some will not be, and instead of enabling a chance of incurring the instances that are not bona fide, the better approach is to cut-off the option altogether.

In essence, beyond "never allowed" is a perceived slippery slope and thus the notion is to not allow any slippage potential at all, thus, stand fast on the precept that an officer should never ever shoot at a moving vehicle.

You might have recently heard or seen in the media a lot of vigorous dialogue and acrimonious debate about this rather contentious and problematic matter.

Recent news stories about policing have at times mentioned a campaign that is seeking to have police departments adopt eight policies, known as the "8 Can't Wait" code.

One of the steadfast eight rules of the campaign is that officers should be banned from shooting at moving vehicles "in all cases" and that without such a policy there are "loopholes," accordingly shooting at moving vehicles ought to be "categorically banned."

You might be wondering what the law currently indicates about such matters.

Generally, US federal laws and guidelines follow the advisement of several related Supreme Court rulings, each of which tends to ultimately hinge on the meaning of the Fourth Amendment, which you might recall states this: "The right of the people to be secure in their persons, houses, papers, and effects, against unreasonable searches and seizures, shall not be violated, and no warrants shall issue, but upon probable cause, supported by oath or affirmation, and particularly describing the place to be searched, and the persons or things to be seized."

In a 1985 ruling by the Supreme Court in the case of Tennessee v. Garner, and as it pertains to the Fourth Amendment meaning, a decision was rendered that if "the officer has probable cause to believe that the suspect poses a significant threat of death or serious physical injury to the officer or others," the officer can use deadly force to prevent an escape by the suspect, but otherwise cannot do so when such conditions otherwise do not exist.

In short, this is a variant of the "allowed rarely if ever" and/or the "allowed in due course as merited" approaches, and decidedly is not the "never allowed" approach.

Other relevant Supreme Court decisions include Graham v. Connor (1989), Plumhoff v. Rickard (2014), Mullenix v. Luma (2015), and other such cases, all of which further refined or reinforced the key characteristics associated with the "allowed" circumstances.

Meanwhile, each of the states has at times opted to stipulate their own rules on the matter, presumably doing so in alignment with the overarching perspective rendered by the US Supreme Court.

Notice that the states can opt to adopt a "never allowed" rule if they wish to do so.

Furthermore, complicating the situation to some degree, there are approximately 18,000 law enforcement bodies throughout the US, and they too can stipulate their own rules, as long as they do so within the presumed bounds of their state rule and the US Supreme Court rulings.

The result has been criticized as an unwieldy mishmash.

Some police departments have adopted the "never allowed," while others have adopted the "allowed" variants. Plus, over time, there are police departments that have shifted in the adoption of the rules and gone from one of the approaches to another one of the approaches.

This would seem to suggest that there are valid arguments to be made for whichever approach is chosen, though those within any particular approach are apt to strongly argue that theirs is the only truly valid approach and the others are plainly wrong.

Some though are conflicted and opt for a given approach, hopeful that it is the "best" choice in hand, and yet are willing to reconsider based on how things bear out, having a willingness to be open to change if changing seems worthwhile.

You might be wondering why there is such disparate opinion about the subject.

Let's do a brief dive into the matter and see.

The Complexities Of Shooting At A Moving Vehicle

Unlike what you might see in the movies, shooting at a moving vehicle is not a simple action.

First, consider that a moving vehicle can be essentially a multi-ton deadly weapon in of itself. The vehicle can be used by a driver to rundown people, or smash into other cars, or ram into objects, etc.

Second, the driver of the moving vehicle might themselves be armed directly with a deadly weapon, perhaps possessing a handgun or brandishing their firearm, possibly even firing the weapon at those outside the vehicle, or threatening to shoot someone else within the vehicle.

In essence, there is a potential dual-threat, the threat of using the vehicle as a deadly weapon, and the threat potential of the driver being armed and using their weapon for deadly purposes too.

Suppose a police officer is standing in front of the vehicle and it is being driven in such a way that the driver appears to be intending to run over the officer.

Can the police officer use their firearm to try and shoot the driver?

In theory, the shooting of the driver will prevent the driver from running down the officer. But, trying to shoot and hit a driver that is in a moving vehicle is not a sure thing, and again not akin to what you see in movies and TV shows.

Some point out that the shots by the officer could hit and harm others inside the vehicle that might be either not bent on the apparent attempt to run over the officer or that are perhaps innocents that have been kidnapped essentially by the driver.

The shots could also ricochet or miss entirely and hit innocent bystanders.

Besides, even if the driver is hit by shots, the driver might still be able to drive the car, or they will be incapacitated and unable to drive, for which the car might then barrel out-of-control as a kind of now misguided weapon, perhaps running over bystanders, etc.

Perhaps the officer should be shooting at the vehicle, attempting to disable the car, rather than shooting at the driver, since the car itself is a bigger target and more likely able to be struck.

This is not quite as ready as a solution as you might assume. Conventional police firearms are not particularly likely to penetrate the vehicle sufficiently to somehow stop the engine or halt the car, and for those that think the tires should be shot out, it is much harder to flatten today's tires by a bullet than might seem to be portrayed in fictional films.

As a counter-argument to the possibility of the officer's bullets missing their intended target, those that are in the sometimes-allowed approach would likely say that if there is a chance to prevent the driver from otherwise killing or injuring people, it would seem a potentially worthwhile effort, and the situation at hand might in the balance save lives by the officer taking such actions.

Generally, there are lots of probabilities and uncertainties involved.

The "never allowed" perspective asserts that police officers should not be making those kinds of judgments and instead should consider taking some other action, but not be shooting at the vehicle.

Indeed, there is some that question why an officer allowed themselves to get into a posture that the driver can viably threaten to run them down, or that the officer can merely jump out of the path of the vehicle.

Others though counter-argue that it is not realistic to think that an officer would always be able to avoid getting caught in such a predicament, plus the viewpoint that the officer should just leap out of the way is exceedingly farfetched and not realistic.

The scenario of the officer getting rundown is only one sliver of the circumstances that might arise for those that are in the sometimes-allowed viewpoint.

Suppose the driver is steering toward the sidewalk and some pedestrians will likely get struck and rundown.

In this case, the officer might not be in imminent danger, but those innocent bystanders are.

Can the police officer use their firearm to try and shoot the driver?

When presented with this type of an example, many would oftentimes find themselves struggling to remain in the never-allowed rule, since they see the tradeoff of having the officer shoot to try and prevent a larger potential set of deaths, even if it means that the shots fired by the officer go astray or do not end-up preventing the mayhem, at least an attempt was made and had a chance of curtailing the full extent of the injury and deaths that might have ensued.

Notice too that these are usually life-or-death moments and must be acted upon in real-time, meaning that there is at times little or no time to consider all options and the uncertainties underlying them.

Ironically, one supposes, this lack of time and sense of urgency can be used by either side of the argument, namely the never-allowed stating that a spur of the moment decision should not be permitted, while the sometimes-allowed would argue that it showcases the need for flexibility and reliance upon the officer in-the-moment making a crucial possibly life-saving decision.

For any such situations whereby the officer might have acted in a life-saving manner, the never-allowed will typically counter-argue that this needs to be weighed against the instances of officers that miscomprehend the situation and make a wrongful choice, and also those instances in which "bad actor" officers opt to exploit the situation and make an intentionally aberrant choice that is intending for harm and was not warranted by the circumstances.

So far, we've not yet considered herein the facet of a driver that is shooting while driving the vehicle, which would certainly tend to up the ante on the use of dual deadly weapons.

A slew of other considerations might come to play.

Suppose the driver was known to have a criminal record that included the use of deadly force.

Suppose the driver is smashing into other cars and threatening the lives of people in those other vehicles.

Suppose a car chase is underway. Some would argue that there is no need to undergo a car chase and just let the driver proceed, catching the driver at some future occasion, though the counter-argument is that the driver might be prone to harming others in the interim to whenever they might later be caught.

Round and round the arguments go.

Another twist that is a doozie involves the use of a car as a weapon of mass destruction (WMD).

Suppose the car is jampacked with explosives.

The driver might be seeking to use the car as more than a ramming device and be intending to cause a large amount of abhorrent destruction. Furthermore, it could be that the driver is willing to die in the act of doing so, being a suicide bomber, as it were.

Can the police officer use their firearm to try and shoot the driver?

This question overall about a police officer shooting at a moving vehicle is a daunting one and remains elusively unresolved by society.

Self-Driving Cars As A New Case

Shift gears and consider that we are gradually going to witness the advent of self-driving cars.

Here's an intriguing question: *How will AI-based true self-driving cars alter our viewpoints about the act of a police officer shooting at a moving vehicle?*

Let's unpack the matter and see.

First, as clarification, true self-driving cars are ones that the AI drives the car entirely on its own and there isn't any human assistance during the driving task.

These driverless vehicles are considered a Level 4 and Level 5, while a car that requires a human driver to co-share the driving effort is usually considered at a Level 2 or Level 3. The cars that co-share the driving task are described as being semi-autonomous, and typically contain a variety of automated add-on's that are referred to as ADAS (Advanced Driver-Assistance Systems).

There is not yet a true self-driving car at Level 5, which we don't yet even know if this will be possible to achieve, and nor how long it will take to get there.

Meanwhile, the Level 4 efforts are gradually trying to get some traction by undergoing very narrow and selective public roadway trials, though there is controversy over whether this testing should be allowed per se.

Since semi-autonomous cars require a human driver, the adoption of those types of cars won't be markedly different than driving conventional vehicles, so there's not much new per se to cover about them on this topic (though, as you'll see in a moment, the points next made are generally applicable).

For semi-autonomous cars, it is important that the public needs to be forewarned about a disturbing aspect that's been arising lately, namely that despite those human drivers that keep posting videos of themselves falling asleep at the wheel of a Level 2 or Level 3 car, we all need to avoid being misled into believing that the driver can take away their attention from the driving task while driving a semi-autonomous car.

You are the responsible party for the driving actions of the vehicle, regardless of how much automation might be tossed into a Level 2 or Level 3.

Self-Driving Cars And Shooting At A Moving Vehicle

For Level 4 and Level 5 true self-driving vehicles, there won't be a human driver involved in the driving task.

All occupants will be passengers.

The AI is doing the driving.

Upon initial thought, you might assume that since there isn't a human driver, there would never be a need to consider shooting at a self-driving car.

Maybe yes, maybe no.

Suppose that a passenger inside a self-driving car has a gun and is shooting at bystanders.

Can the police officer use their firearm to try and shoot the passenger?

It seems that we are not going to avoid the question, even when self-driving cars arrive.

You could use the same arguments as before, asserting that the officer's shots might go astray, and thus you might still argue that the never-allowed is the right rule, or you might be in the sometimes-allowed perspective and indicate that if the circumstances seem applicable that the officer can go ahead and try to shoot the passenger, hopefully striking the passenger and stopping any subsequent carnage caused by the passenger using their weapon.

Some would quickly offer that the AI ought to be told via electronic communication to drive the vehicle to a remote spot and thus prevent the shooting passenger from harming anyone.

Well, that might work, but who will send such a directive, and meanwhile what about the passenger that is nonetheless still shooting at bystanders during that suggested journey?

For more details about the controversies and tradeoffs in how to redirect or stop self-driving cars by authorities when perceived as so needed.

Recall that earlier we had acknowledged that there is a dual weapon possibility, namely that the driver (now a passenger) could have a weapon, and likewise, the car itself could be used as a weapon.

Does the advent of self-driving cars at least though obviate the concerns about the self-driving car itself being used as a deadly weapon?

It might seem unthinkable that a self-driving car could somehow be used as a weapon in of itself. You would undoubtedly assume that the on-board AI system would be programmed to avoid hitting people and other cars, such that the AI would not allow the vehicle to be a weapon per se.

One supposes that if an officer stood in front of a self-driving car, it would dutifully automatically come to a halt or otherwise avoid hitting the officer, and therefore the car itself would no longer be actionable as a weapon.

Numerous scenarios belie that simplicity.

Suppose a self-driving car is going on the freeway at 65 miles per hour, there is a passenger shooting from within the vehicle, and it is known that the car is packed with explosives.

The self-driving car is indeed now a weapon, though the AI is not aware of this.

Note that today's AI does not have any semblance of common-sense reasoning, it is not sentient, and the odds of the singularity happening anytime soon is slim at best, so do not assume that the AI driving system will be all-knowing.

In short, the emergence of AI-based true self-driving cars is going to be encumbered by the same realities that we face today with conventional cars, though indubitably with a different set of twists and turns (including, for example, shooting at a self-driving car that has no passengers at all, which offers its own set of conundrums).

Conclusion

Most of the automakers and self-driving car tech firms would likely argue that this whole matter is an edge or corner case, meaning that it will rarely occur and does not need attention at this time, especially since they are immersed in just getting self-driving cars to drive in everyday circumstances safely.

Unfortunately, the real-world will ultimately catch-up with the extraordinary innovation of self-driving cars, and we will collectively need to answer some troubling and difficult ethical questions.

The advent of AI does not necessarily overcome tough ethical dilemmas and without doubt, has the potential for bringing new ones to the forefront.

CHAPTER 7
US FEDERAL TESTING LOG
AND
AI SELF-DRIVING CARS

CHAPTER 7

US FEDERAL TESTING LOG

AND

AI SELF-DRIVING CARS

The U.S. federally chartered automotive safety agency NHTSA (National Highway Traffic Safety Administration) has announced today a new online log that will be used to indicate the ongoing status of nationwide Autonomous Vehicles (AVs) public roadway efforts, including those of self-driving cars.

Known as the AV TEST initiative, a catchy acronym for Automated Vehicle Transparency and Engagement for Safe Testing, the public will be able to see the log online and also sign-up to be emailed whenever the latest info is posted.

As stated at the AV TEST website: "You'll be able to see if testing has been reported in your community and learn more about the types of activities happening, including testing of various types of motor vehicles — cars, low-speed shuttles, trucks, and driverless electric delivery vehicles."

Speakers at today's kick-off included U.S. Department of Transportation Secretary Elaine L. Chao, National Highway Traffic Safety Administration Deputy Administrator James C. Owens, Federal Highway Administration Administrator Nicole Nason, and U.S. DOT Deputy Assistant Secretary for Transportation Policy Finch Fulton.

Rightfully, the session emphasized that there are not yet today any true self-driving cars yet available for sale to the public and that it is important to clarify the difference between semi-autonomous vehicles and those that are fully autonomous. As eloquently stated by NHTSA Deputy Administrator James Owens: "For starters, there are no vehicles with automated driving systems available for sale to the public today, any vehicle that public can buy today cannot drive itself. It requires an active attentive and fully engaged driver, ready to act."

I'll say more about this in a moment.

One crucial caveat to keep in mind is that the log is based on voluntary submissions from those that are fielding self-driving vehicles, which means that the automakers and self-driving car firms can opt to post their status or decide to do not so.

Furthermore, when they post their status, it could presumably be quite outdated and not necessarily reflect their most recent activities.

Nonetheless, providing a centralized and easily utilized log is hopefully going to be well received and appropriately used on a timely and effective basis by all.

This is especially welcomed on a centralized basis since currently the myriad of states that are enabling self-driving vehicle testing are widely disparate in their reporting efforts. Some states have required annual reporting, some states lack any viable reporting, and it is an across the board mishmash that can be laborious to try and stay on top of.

So far, purportedly nine companies have signed-up to use the new AV TEST log including Fiat Chrysler, Toyota Motor, Cruise, Local Motors, Navya, Uber Technologies Inc., Nuro, Beep, and Waymo.

One nifty feature of the AV TEST will be an online mapping tool that will allow the public to zoom-in on where public roadway testing efforts are taking place, allowing you to ascertain if self-driving vehicles are roaming your neck of the woods, as it were. Also, data such as the type of vehicles being used, their frequency of use, dates of use, routes being taken, and other related info will be potentially available via the log.

And, reportedly eight states have signed-up to-date to use the new log including California, Florida, Maryland, Michigan, Ohio, Pennsylvania, Texas, and Utah.

The reason that the state and local agencies might log data at the AV TEST site is to indicate what types of legislation are being employed in their realm to oversee self-driving testing, and might also include aspects about emergency response plans if any self-driving adverse events occur.

For overall info about what the U.S. Department of Transportation (USDOT) is doing regarding AVs, including a series of notable policy statements, the latest being AV 4.0 entitled "Ensuring American Leadership in Automated Vehicle Technologies: Automated Vehicles 4.0" see the USDOT website.

Meanwhile, please be aware that federal legislation about regulating self-driving cars has continued to be stalled in Congress, partially due to differing viewpoints across political lines and most recently as a result of the pandemic and a focus on other legislative matters.

It would seem unlikely that any such legislation will be completed soon, especially with the November election coming up, thus don't expect to have new federal regulations on AVs until at least sometime next year.

There are some arguing fervently that more laws and regulations are needed to keep the self-driving industry on point and ensure that the vaunted mobility-for-all aspiration will be achieved, along with attempting to implement stronger safety measures than otherwise might be chosen by the industry.

At the same time, some want to change the existing laws that are seen as hampering progress in self-driving cars, thus proclaimed to be delaying the mobility-for-all hopes and impeding the presumed reduction in lives lost due to human-driven efforts.

The shape and nature of what such legislation should consist of have been a long-standing tug-of-war and will likely remain so until other exigencies might occur.

Understanding The Levels Of Self-Driving Cars

As a clarification, true self-driving cars are ones that the AI drives the car entirely on its own and there isn't any human assistance during the driving task.

These driverless vehicles are considered a Level 4 and Level 5, while a car that requires a human driver to co-share the driving effort is usually considered at a Level 2 or Level 3. The cars that co-share the driving task are described as being semi-autonomous, and typically contain a variety of automated add-on's that are referred to as ADAS (Advanced Driver-Assistance Systems).

There is not yet a true self-driving car at Level 5, which we don't yet even know if this will be possible to achieve, and nor how long it will take to get there.

Meanwhile, the Level 4 efforts are gradually trying to get some traction by undergoing very narrow and selective public roadway trials, though there is controversy over whether this testing should be allowed per se.

Since semi-autonomous cars require a human driver, the adoption of those types of cars won't be markedly different than driving conventional vehicles, so there's not much new per se to cover about them on this topic (though, as you'll see in a moment, the points next made are generally applicable).

For semi-autonomous cars, it is important that the public needs to be forewarned about a disturbing aspect that's been arising lately, namely that despite those human drivers that keep posting videos of themselves falling asleep at the wheel of a Level 2 or Level 3 car, we all need to avoid being misled into believing that the driver can take away their attention from the driving task while driving a semi-autonomous car.

You are the responsible party for the driving actions of the vehicle, regardless of how much automation might be tossed into a Level 2 or Level 3.

For Level 4 and Level 5 true self-driving vehicles, there won't be a human driver involved in the driving task.

All occupants will be passengers.

The AI is doing the driving.

Potential For Media Misreporting

Shifting gears, it is handy to consider what might take place as a result of the new AV TEST log.

Sadly, one segment that might not use the log appropriately could be the media, going astray in misreporting whatever might be posted at the log, and, potentially misreporting what is even <u>not</u> posted there too.

For example, already a media report indicated that the AV TEST log would indicate where Apple self-driving cars are being tested.

This is a smattering of unseemly shenanigans.

While it is true that Apple might opt to report as such, there is no requirement that they do so, and we will have to wait-and-see what Apple chooses to do. It is already the case that Apple has been quite tightlipped about their efforts and one wonders whether they will voluntarily share info about their heretofore quite secretive activities on self-driving cars.

Another potential boondoggle will be the potential reporting and misreporting by the media about disengagements.

Essentially, disengagements are supposed to be instances of when a self-driving car being tested on public roadways was taken over by an on-board human backup driver. The backup driver might decide that the AI driving system is about to make a mistake and thus choose to grab the driving controls back from the self-driving system. Or, the AI itself might detect a circumstance that requires the human backup driver to handle a thorny driving situation and handover the driving accordingly.

The media oftentimes misstates the significance and nature of disengagements, doing so in a variety of ill-informed and at times oddly creative ways.

One such method consists of ranking the self-driving efforts by the number of reported disengagements, implying that the tryouts with the least number of disengagements must ergo be further along and more advanced than those that have a higher number of disengagements.

Here's why that is misleading, at best.

Suppose firm X has 5 disengagements and firm Y has had 20. Seemingly, if reported simply on that basis, it would appear that firm X is doing much better by far than firm Y.

But suppose that firm X has driven only 100 miles, while firm Y has driven 10,000 miles, I think you can readily realize that the number of disengagements per miles driven would be a lot less for firm Y, suggesting that firm Y is doing much better than firm X.

Even this though is problematic.

As is well-known in the self-driving industry, all miles are not the same.

If a company opts to undertake their public tryouts in a quiet suburban neighborhood, those miles driven would presumably be relatively "easy" miles, assuming that there is likely not much vehicular traffic and the driving situations are tame.

In comparison, public tryouts in a hectic downtown city with bustling traffic, dealing with jaywalking pedestrians and wild drivers, these are decidedly not the same kinds of miles as those of a somewhat docile suburban setting.

On top of all of those considerations is that disengagements can be somewhat tricked.

If you are leery of having to report your disengagements, one approach would be to tell the backup drivers to refrain from undertaking a disengagement, nearly at all costs, to keep your counts lowered.

In that sense, a reporting aspect can inadvertently spur adverse behavior, ironically so, since the original intent might have been noble and seeking to find out how safely the self-driving vehicles are performing but it got mired in misreporting and maligned use.

In short, please be on the watch for "fake news" about self-driving cars.

And the AV TEST log will likely spark more such misleading and mistaken reporting.

Conclusion

Do not misinterpret this to suggest that having such a nationwide log is somehow unwelcomed.

A log can be quite useful and hopefully will be used properly to stimulate discussion and stoke a healthy and vigorous debate about the status and future of self-driving vehicles.

Perhaps the fact that the log is publicly being posted might aid in overstepping those media that provide a misinterpretation or entail some other skewed viewpoint. All of us will be able to inspect the log and reach our own conclusions.

Furthermore, perhaps the pressures from other media that do report properly will weigh on those that do not do so.

On top of that, there is a chance that the automakers and self-driving car firms will be inspired to do the reporting as a result of media reporting. In other words, if a firm decides to not share their info in the AV TEST log, media reporting will point out this omission and ramp-up pressure on the company to start making their data publicly available.

Of course, the bad apples of reporting might discourage some firms from sharing their info, and be pointed to as an indication of why voluntarily reporting is just as troubling as not doing so, given that whatever is shared could be misstated or miscast.

In the end, hopefully, the new AV TEST log will be usefully utilized by all parties and we'll be collectively glad that such a log exists.

Time will tell.

CHAPTER 8

DRIVE-BY SHOOTINGS
AND
AI SELF-DRIVING CARS

Dr. Lance B. Eliot

CHAPTER 8

DRIVE-BY SHOOTINGS

AND

AI SELF-DRIVING CARS

Drive-by shootings continue to be in the news and seem to be occurring at an alarming pace.

Those that undertake this heinous act are often doing so on the basis that they believe they will not be caught.

Here's why they believe so.

Via a car, it is possible to be somewhat hidden within the vehicle, not especially noticeable from the outside, and rapidly approach wherever the perpetrator intends to fire a shot, along with having a speedy getaway after shooting at their target.

All in all, a car provides several crucial elements in the performance of a drive-by shooting.

The car is a kind of protector.

It helps to disguise or hide the perpetrator. A targeted person does not necessarily realize that the car holds someone desiring to shoot at them. Also, if the fired at intended target attempts to shoot back at the shooter, once the initial shots are fired, the car acts as a type of shield.

Thus, a car is handy as a means of committing a drive-by shooting since it provides a form of protective cover.

The car aids in rapidly committing the drive-by act.

Speed in the case of drive-by shootings is frequently a key tactic that the perpetrator relies upon. If they were slowly approaching the intended target on say foot, they might be discovered, and a preemptive strike might occur, or the target might have time to hide or flee. After the perpetrator takes a shot, they could get rushed in response, but with a car, they can quickly drive away from the scene.

The car can be said to bolster the perpetrator in a willingness to do a drive-by shooting.

Those that commit a drive-by shooting are potentially bolstered by being inside a car, feeling less vulnerable, and gaining a sense of anonymity that no one will necessarily know that they committed the crime. In some cases, the perpetrator purposely pokes their head out of the car to let the intended target know it is them, yet assumes doing so will only reveal themselves to the victim and not otherwise readily showcase their criminal activity to other potential eyewitnesses.

Statistics about drive-by shootings are somewhat sporadically recorded and not especially thoroughly logged on a nationwide basis.

A prior study that examined drive-by shooting counts came to some interesting and tentative indications (be careful in using these results since it was a point-in-time study and other limitations apply), including:

- About half of drive-by shootings occurred at a targeted residence
- Other locales included street corners, parking lots, basketball courts, bus stops, etc.
- Drive-by shootings tended to occur at nighttime, usually between 7 p.m. and midnight
- Peak months were in the summertime, lowest months in the winter
- Gang involvement was a common underlying aspect

Generally, those identified characteristics seem to make intuitive sense, namely that a drive-by shooting would tend to be done at nighttime, providing the added cover of darkness, and more so during the summer months, when people are outdoors, and that the location would be near a residence which presumably is where the target is known to be or likely to live, along with other locations that might be prime places to spot the intended victim.

The listed Top 10 ranked states for overall counts of drive-by shootings were noted as (from most to less):
- California
- Texas
- Florida
- Illinois
- Washington (tied with Illinois)
- Oklahoma
- North Carolina
- Georgia
- New York
- Louisiana

Some states have laws specifically directed at drive-by shootings, providing a particular indication about nature and repercussions associated with this decidedly illegal act.

Besides the harm to an intended victim, a drive-by shooting is bound to potentially incur collateral damage, possibly striking innocent bystanders. The shooter might fire multiple rounds, doing so on a scattergun manner in hopes of striking the intended target and horrifically those rounds might find their way to hitting bystanders.

An additional reason for the bullets hitting others is that the shooter inside a car is presumably not able to as readily aim at their intended target, having to do so from inside the vehicle, and even when outstretching an arm to try and use the firearm slightly outside the interior of the car, the result is likely to be poorly aimed (the shooter is undoubtedly nervous and anxious too, effecting any accurate discharge of the firearm).

The car is usually in motion, though perhaps having slowed down, yet nonetheless adds another confounding factor in being able to aim precisely at the victim, as does the potential distance to the target since the car is most likely on the roadway and the target is some distance from the street (which, also explains why the instances of a bus stop or street corner are sometimes used, providing a closer-in target).

Why do people do drive-by shootings?

One obvious intent is gang-related.

A rival of a gang might seek to shoot someone in a targeted gang. Trying to get near to the intended target by walking up to them could be difficult, perhaps due to being surrounded by a protective force of fellow gang members, and thus a quick drive-by seems to offer a chance of catching the victim off-guard and allowing too for an escape without harm.

The drive-by shooting might be intended to kill, yet only end-up injuring the victim or might be intending to injure and yet result in killing the victim (or others).

Drive-by shootings will frequently lead to a retributive act, and therefore one drive-by shooting can spark a spate of subsequent drive-by shootings by each side, in turn. This provides a kind of multiplier and can in a sense socially and virally trigger a series of drive-by shooting efforts.

Other reasons that people do drive-by shootings include being on drugs or drunk and opting to do a drive-by shooting while impaired, perhaps feeling strengthened in doing so due to the intoxication.

A drive-by shooting might be planned and carefully performed, or it could be ad hoc and occur on the spur of the moment. There are instances of sudden road rage whereby a driver of a vehicle got upset at another driver or a pedestrian and pulled out a gun to take a shot at the perceived offender.

The intended target might have been singled out or could be someone randomly chosen.

The law typically considers whether the drive-by shooting was willfully performed and whether it was maliciously conducted.

At times, the shooter is the driver, taking on both roles, while in other cases there is a driver, while the shooter is strictly a passenger. In theory, a passenger doing the shooting is less encumbered since they are not tasked with driving and might be more able to target the victim.

All told, this brings us to a final overarching point and important question, notably why a drive-by shooter is not necessarily caught, either at the time of the shooting or subsequently thereafter (again, stats are hard to come by on the odds of getting caught, which it seems when gangs are involved tends to be less likely, since a rival gang is presumably not likely to report the incident).

You might rightfully assume that a perpetrator ought to be somewhat readily caught, for the simple reason that they are using a car to commit the crime. One would assume that the use of a car would have a downside in that the car itself is a means to figure out the potential identity of the shooter.

A car is a large object, very noticeable, and probably has a license plate too.

Those witnessing a drive-by shooting are usually able to vaguely describe the vehicle, perhaps indicating the make and model, along with other aspects such as the paint color and so on, but are not as likely to have fully spotted the license number.

This lack of being able to discern the license plate makes sense, given the rush of the moment and the surprising jolt of witnessing a shooting take place, and that the license itself might be hard to see or partially obscured on purpose.

Shift gears for a moment.

Suppose that there was a better way to detect and track when a drive-by shooting occurred.

Imagine an improved method or approach of detection and tracking that might significantly undercut the assumption by perpetrators that they are bound to get away with this atrocious act.

This could cause drive-by shootings to lessen.

What such means might there be?

Consider this interesting question: *Will the advent of AI-based true self-driving cars be a deterrent to the act of drive-by shootings and potentially lessen or curtail this scourge?*

Let's unpack the matter and see.

Understanding The Levels Of Self-Driving Cars

As a clarification, AI-based true self-driving cars are ones that the AI drives the car entirely on its own and there isn't any human assistance during the driving task.

These driverless vehicles are considered a Level 4 and Level 5, while a car that requires a human driver to co-share the driving effort is usually considered at a Level 2 or Level 3. The cars that co-share the driving task are described as being semi-autonomous, and typically contain a variety of automated add-on's that are referred to as ADAS (Advanced Driver-Assistance Systems).

There is not yet a true self-driving car at Level 5, which we don't yet even know if this will be possible to achieve, and nor how long it will take to get there.

Meanwhile, the Level 4 efforts are gradually trying to get some traction by undergoing very narrow and selective public roadway trials, though there is controversy over whether this testing should be allowed per se.

Since semi-autonomous cars require a human driver, the adoption of those types of cars won't be markedly different than driving conventional vehicles, so there's not much new per se to cover about them on this topic (though, as you'll see in a moment, the points next made are generally applicable).

For semi-autonomous cars, it is important that the public needs to be forewarned about a disturbing aspect that's been arising lately, namely that despite those human drivers that keep posting videos of themselves falling asleep at the wheel of a Level 2 or Level 3 car, we all need to avoid being misled into believing that the driver can take away their attention from the driving task while driving a semi-autonomous car.

You are the responsible party for the driving actions of the vehicle, regardless of how much automation might be tossed into a Level 2 or Level 3.

Self-Driving Cars And Drive-By Shootings

For Level 4 and Level 5 true self-driving vehicles, there won't be a human driver involved in the driving task.

All occupants will be passengers.

The AI is doing the driving.

Let's return to the question about drive-by shootings.

Your first thought might be that there will never be any drive-by shootings again since one shudders to think that the amazing innovation of true self-driving cars would be used in such an underhanded and foul manner.

Sorry to say, drive-by shootings are not quite fully obviated simply due to the emergence of self-driving cars.

Keep in mind too that it will take many years, likely decades, for self-driving cars to gradually be rolled-out on any massive scale, thus for a long time to come there will be a mixture of human-driven cars and self-driving cars. This suggests that human-driven cars will still be utilized, and they can continue to be part of those despicable drive-by shootings.

Focus next exclusively on self-driving cars.

Could a dastardly person use a self-driving car to commit a drive-by shooting?

Sure, why not.

Consider the following scenario.

A person with a concealed gun in their jacket pocket gets into a self-driving car and calmly instructs the AI to drive to a particular destination, making use of the in-car Natural Language Processing (NLP) system capabilities, similar to using today's Alexa or Siri.

It is anticipated that the AI driving system will allow passengers to also specify waypoints, such as visiting the grocery store on the way to seeing their relatives.

The evildoer with the gun could tell the AI to drive past a specific residence or street corner or wherever so desired, doing this would not raise any undue suspicion for the AI system and would simply be an expected part of any typical driving journey.

Upon getting near to the destination, the shooter might ask the AI to slow down, and then, merely open the car window and take a shot at whatever target they have in mind.

After doing so, the shooter might request the AI to speed-up and head quickly to wherever their getaway location is.

Note that the shooter isn't driving the car and therefore is solely in the role of being a passenger, meaning too that they perhaps are more able to skillfully aim their shot and not be distracted by the driving task. This aspect is an unfortunate "advantage" for those wishing to use a self-driving car as part of drive-by shooting activity.

Notice too that the shooter might have overtly planned to conduct the drive-by shooting, or they could be generally touting a firearm and have decided to randomly do the shooting, maybe opportunistically based on the perchance moment of seeing someone they wanted to take a shot at.

It is a sad fact that self-driving cars could be used in this appalling way.

When I mention that drive-by shootings could occur while using a self-driving, some are aghast and insist that we ought to not discuss this possibility else it will plant a seed in the minds of those that are bent on drive-by shootings.

Please know that a head-in-the-sand approach is not wise and will simply mean that once people figure out that they can use a self-driving car for such a purpose, everyone will be caught by surprise and be exceedingly flatfooted as to what to do.

Instead, a more astute approach involves trying to develop and deploy self-driving cars in a manner that will seek to reduce or mitigate the chances of someone undertaking a drive-by shooting while inside a self-driving car.

Let's consider how this can be undertaken.

In the natural course of devising self-driving cars, one already preexistent stopping block is that presumably the AI will not peel out and push the pedal to the floor to screech away from the scene of the shooting. By-and-large, most of the automakers and self-driving tech firms are trying to ensure that the AI drives civilly, and certainly drives within the speed limits.

Someone anticipating doing a drive-by shooting is not going to be able to flee the scene so rapidly as they might have if they or an accomplice were driving in a conventional car.

But they could nonetheless still take a shot, plus they might not even ask the AI to slow down, and the vehicle could be already underway and zipping along at whatever speed limit is allowed.

The point is that the legal driving activity of an AI-based true self-driving car does *not preclude* a drive-by shooting per se, and merely makes it more cumbersome and possibly less alluring to a perpetrator.

There is more though that a self-driving car can be made to do to undermine drive-by shootings.

Most self-driving cars will have inward-facing cameras and an audio system, used to both see and hear the passengers inside the vehicle. This will be likely desirous especially by ride-sharing and rental firms that want to detect whether a passenger has opted to mark graffiti inside the vehicle or perhaps is damaging the seats or interior.

I've repeatedly pointed out that this will raise contentious privacy questions, including how such video recordings might be used or distributed by the fleet owners of self-driving cars.

In any case, self-driving cars equipped with the inward-facing cameras would seem to be a notable deterrent for any drive-by shooter, since the wrongdoers would be captured on-tape as they commit their shameful act.

This could make drive-shooters think twice before taking such actions.

Of course, the shooter could opt to wear a disguise and might use a fake ID as part of the rental or ride-sharing payment for the use of the self-driving car.

Sadly, where there is a will, there is a way.

Another facet of a self-driving car that could aid in potentially curtailing drive-by shootings has to do with the abundance of state-of-the-art sensors bundled into the self-driving car for driving purposes.

Those sophisticated sensory devices such as specialized cameras, radar, LIDAR, thermal imaging, ultrasonic, and so on, will be continuously scanning the surroundings of the self-driving car. The collected data is used by the AI as its eyes and ears, as it were, for ascertaining where to drive and what to avoid such as other cars and nearby pedestrians.

As a quick aside, this once again opens another privacy can of worms, due to the reality that when a self-driving car goes down your neighborhood street, it is likely recording everything it detects. This can be uploaded into a cloud-based system, via OTA (Over-The-Air) electronic communications, and then stitched together with other data from thousands upon thousands of other self-driving cars.

Your privacy is at risk due to this roving eye.

In any case, what is good or bad for the goose can be equally good or bad for the gander.

The AI could potentially detect that a gun was fired from within the self-driving car (even if an arm was outstretched in doing so), based on a combination of the inward-facing sensors and the outward-facing sensors, and could be recording the act, along with monitoring any such activity in real-time during a driving journey.

Conclusion

What might the AI do?

Nobody has yet pursued this in any detail, and thus right now, the AI would be "oblivious" and not take any notice.

Presumably, if the AI is programmed to detect this kind of activity, it could take any number of actions.

One action would be to immediately contact the police.

Another would be to bring the car to a halt, which would put the shooter in presumed dire straits, and thus they might not want to use a self-driving car due to the realization it is going to leave them at the mercy of their potential prey (this is not necessarily a discouragement per se and a drive-by shooter might have anticipated this accordingly).

The self-driving car would at least have a recording of what took place, which might be useful to authorities when trying to track down the culprit.

Unfortunately, none of these are ironclad ways to prevent a drive-by shooting (some dreamily envision that the car would auto-lock the person in the vehicle and zoom over to the nearest police station, but this is both Utopian and Dystopian at the same time, and not in the cards anytime soon, if ever).

Criminals undoubtedly will be using a cat-and-mouse approach of figuring out ways to try and circumvent the detections and actions of the AI, though this does not mean that we shouldn't put in place as many barriers and hurdles as we can.

Right now, the automakers and self-driving firms have their hands full of just getting self-driving cars to work, safely so, and in everyday uses, though soon enough the real-world will catch-up with self-driving cars and more advanced aspects will need to be devised to cope with matters such as the menace of a drive-by shooting.

Perhaps someday the AI will be sharp enough that it will be able to take an active role in discouraging drive-by shooters, talking them out of their vile acts.

That is an AI for social good that we could all relish.

CHAPTER 9
AI ETHICS KNOBS
AND
AI SELF-DRIVING CARS

CHAPTER 9
AI ETHICS KNOBS AND
AI SELF-DRIVING CARS

AI systems are being churned out at quite a rapid pace, meanwhile, there are considerable qualms about whether such AI will exhibit ethical behavior.

There is a rising tide of concern about AI ethics.

How so?

Consider a real-world example.

Suppose an AI application is developed to assess car loan applicants.

Using Machine Learning (ML) and Deep Learning (DL), the AI system is trained on a trove of data and arrives at some means of choosing among those that it deems are loan worthy and those that are not.

The underlying Artificial Neural Network (ANN) is so computationally complex that there are no apparent means to interpret how it arrives at the decisions being rendered. Also, there is no built-in explainability capability and thus the AI is unable to articulate why it is making the choices that it is undertaking (note: there is a movement toward including XAI, explainable AI components to try and overcome this inscrutability hurdle).

Upon the AI-based loan assessment application being fielded, soon thereafter protests arise by some that assert they were turned down for their car loan due to an improper inclusion of race or gender as a key factor in rendering the negative decision.

At first, the maker of the AI application insists that they did not utilize such factors and professes complete innocence in the matter.

Turns out though that a third-party audit of the AI application reveals that the ML/DL is indeed using race and gender as core characteristics in the car loan assessment process. Deep within the mathematically arcane elements of the neural network, data related to race and gender were intricately woven into the calculations, having been dug out of the initial training dataset provided when the ANN was crafted.

That is an example of how biases can be hidden within an AI system.

And it also showcases that such biases can go otherwise undetected, including that the developers of the AI did not realize that the biases existed and were seemingly confident that they had not done anything to warrant such biases being included.

People affected by the AI application might not realize they are being subjected to such biases. In this example, those being adversely impacted perchance noticed and voiced their concerns, but we are apt to witness a lot of AI that no one will realize they are being subjugated to biases and therefore not able to ring the bell of dismay.

Various AI Ethics principles are being proffered by a wide range of groups and associations, hoping that those crafting AI will take seriously the need to consider embracing AI ethical considerations throughout the life cycle of designing, building, testing, and fielding AI.

I've previously discussed the AI Ethics principles that the Vatican released and those of the U.S. Department of Defense, and have also described those of the OECD, which consist briefly of these five core precepts:

1) Inclusive growth, sustainable development, and well-being
2) Human-centered values and fairness
3) Transparency and explainability
4) Robustness, security, and safety
5) Accountability

We certainly expect humans to exhibit ethical behavior, and thus it seems fitting that we would expect ethical behavior from AI too.

Since the aspirational goal of AI is to provide machines that are the equivalent of human intelligence, being able to presumably embody the same range of cognitive capabilities that humans do, this perhaps suggests that we will only be able to achieve the vaunted goal of AI by including some form of ethics-related component or capacity.

What this means is that if humans encapsulate ethics, which they seem to do, and if AI is trying to achieve what humans are and do, the AI ought to have an infused ethics capability else it would be something less than the desired goal of achieving human intelligence.

You could claim that anyone crafting AI that does not include an ethics facility is undercutting what should be a crucial and integral aspect of any AI system worth its salt.

Of course, trying to achieve the goals of AI is one matter, meanwhile, since we are going to be mired in a world with AI, for our safety and well-being as humans we would rightfully be arguing that AI had better darned abide by ethical behavior, however that might be so achieved.

Now that we've covered that aspect, let's take a moment to ponder the nature of ethics and ethical behavior.

Do humans always behave ethically?

I think we can all readily agree that humans do not necessarily always behave in a strictly ethical manner.

Is ethical behavior by humans able to be characterized solely by whether someone is in an ethically binary state of being, namely either purely ethical versus being wholly unethical?

I would dare say that we cannot always pin down human behavior into two binary-based and mutually exclusive buckets of being ethical or being unethical. The real-world is often much grayer than that and we at times are more likely to assess that someone is doing something ethically questionable, but it is not purely unethical, nor fully ethical.

In a sense, you could assert that human behavior ranges on a spectrum of ethics, at times being fully ethical and ranging toward the bottom of the scale as being wholly and inarguably unethical.

In-between there is a lot of room for how someone ethically behaves.

If you agree that the world is not a binary ethical choice of behaviors that fit only into truly ethical versus solely unethical, you would therefore also presumably be amenable to the notion that there is a potential scale upon which we might be able to rate ethical behavior.

This scale might be from the scores of 1 to 10, or maybe 1 to 100, or whatever numbering we might wish to try and assign, maybe even including negative numbers too.

Let's assume for the moment that we will use the positive numbers of a 1 to 10 scale for increasingly being ethical (the topmost is 10), and the scores of -1 to -10 for being unethical (the -10 is the least ethical or in other words most unethical potential rating), and zero will be the midpoint of the scale.

Please do not get hung up on the scale numbering, which can be anything else that you might like. We could even use letters of the alphabet or any kind of sliding scale. The point being made is that there is a scale and we could devise some means to establish a suitable scale for use in these matters.

The twist is about to come, so hold onto your hat.

We could observe a human and rate their ethical behavior on particular aspects of what they do. Maybe at work, a person gets an 8 for being ethically observant, while perhaps at home they are a more devious person and they get a -5 score.

Okay, so we can rate human behavior.

Could we drive or guide human behavior by the use of the scale?

Suppose we tell someone that at work they are being observed and their target goal is to hit an ethics score of 9 for their first year with the company. Presumably, they will undertake their work activities in such a way that it helps them to achieve that score.

In that sense, yes, we can potentially guide or prod human behavior by providing targets related to ethical expectations.

I told you a twist was going to arise, and now here it is.

For AI, we could use an ethical rating or score to try and assess how ethically proficient the AI is.

In that manner, we might be more comfortable using that particular AI if we knew that it had a reputable ethical score.

And we could also presumably seek to guide or drive the AI toward an ethical score too, similar to how this can be done with humans, and perhaps indicate that the AI should be striving towards some upper bound on the ethics scale.

Some pundits immediately recoil at this notion.

They argue that AI should always be a +10 (using the scale that I've laid out herein). Anything less than a top ten is an abomination and the AI ought to not exist.

Well, this takes us back into the earlier discussion about whether ethical behavior is in a binary state.

Are we going to hold AI to a "higher bar" than humans by insisting that AI always be "perfectly" ethical and nothing less so?

This is somewhat of a quandary due to the point that AI overall is presumably aiming to be the equivalent of human intelligence, and yet we do not hold humans to that same standard.

For some, they fervently believe that AI must be held to a higher standard than humans. We must not accept or allow any AI that cannot do so.

Others indicate that this seems to fly in the face of what is known about human behavior and begs the question of whether AI can be attained if it must do something that humans cannot attain.

Furthermore, they might argue that forcing AI to do something that humans do not undertake is now veering away from the assumed goal of arriving at the equivalent of human intelligence, which might bump us away from being able to do so as a result of this insistence about ethics.

Round and round these debates continue to go.

Those on the must-be topnotch ethical AI are often quick to point out that by allowing AI to be anything less than a top ten, you are opening Pandora's box. For example, it could be that AI dips down into the negative numbers and sits at a -4, or worse too it digresses to become miserably and fully unethical at a dismal -10.

Anyway, this is a debate that is going to continue and not be readily resolved, so let's move on.

If you are still of the notion that ethics exists on a scale and that AI might also be measured by such a scale, and if you also are willing to accept that behavior can be driven or guided by offering where to reside on the scale, the time is ripe to bring up tuning knobs.

Ethics tuning knobs.

Here's how that works.

You come in contact with an AI system and are interacting with it.

The AI presents you with an ethics tuning knob, showcasing a scale akin to our ethics scale earlier proposed.

Suppose the knob is currently at a 6, but you want the AI to be acting more aligned with an 8, so you turn the knob upward to the 8.

At that juncture, the AI adjusts its behavior so that ethically it is exhibiting an 8-score level of ethical compliance rather than the earlier setting of a 6.

What do you think of that?

Some would bellow out balderdash, hogwash, and just unadulterated nonsense.

A preposterous idea or is it genius?

You'll find that there are experts on both sides of that coin.

Perhaps it might be helpful to provide the ethics tuning knob within a contextual exemplar to highlight how it might come to play.

Here's a handy contextual indication for you: *Will AI-based true self-driving cars potentially contain an ethics tuning knob for use by riders or passengers that use self-driving vehicles?*

Let's unpack the matter and see.

Understanding The Levels Of Self-Driving Cars

As a clarification, true self-driving cars are ones that the AI drives the car entirely on its own and there isn't any human assistance during the driving task.

These driverless vehicles are considered a Level 4 and Level 5 while a car that requires a human driver to co-share the driving effort is usually considered at a Level 2 or Level 3. The cars that co-share the driving task are described as being semi-autonomous, and typically contain a variety of automated add-on's that are referred to as ADAS (Advanced Driver-Assistance Systems).

There is not yet a true self-driving car at Level 5, which we don't yet even know if this will be possible to achieve, and nor how long it will take to get there.

Meanwhile, the Level 4 efforts are gradually trying to get some traction by undergoing very narrow and selective public roadway trials, though there is controversy over whether this testing should be allowed per se.

Since semi-autonomous cars require a human driver, the adoption of those types of cars won't be markedly different than driving conventional vehicles, so there's not much new per se to cover about them on this topic (though, as you'll see in a moment, the points next made are generally applicable).

For semi-autonomous cars, it is important that the public needs to be forewarned about a disturbing aspect that's been arising lately, namely that despite those human drivers that keep posting videos of themselves falling asleep at the wheel of a Level 2 or Level 3 car, we all need to avoid being misled into believing that the driver can take away their attention from the driving task while driving a semi-autonomous car.

You are the responsible party for the driving actions of the vehicle, regardless of how much automation might be tossed into a Level 2 or Level 3.

Self-Driving Cars And Ethics Tuning Knobs

For Level 4 and Level 5 true self-driving vehicles, there won't be a human driver involved in the driving task.

All occupants will be passengers.

The AI is doing the driving.

This seems rather straightforward. You might be wondering where any semblance of ethics behavior enters the picture.

Here's how.

Some believe that a self-driving car should always strictly obey the speed limit.

Imagine that you have just gotten into a self-driving car in the morning and it turns out that you are possibly going to be late getting to work. Your boss is a stickler and has told you that coming in late is a surefire way to get fired.

You tell the AI via its Natural Language Processing (NLP) that the destination is your work address.

And, you ask the AI to hit the gas, push the pedal to the metal, screech those tires, and get you to work on-time.

But it is clear cut that if the AI obeys the speed limit, there is absolutely no chance of arriving at work on-time, and since the AI is only and always going to go at or less than the speed limit, your goose is fried.

Better luck at your next job.

Whoa, suppose the AI driving system had an ethics tuning knob.

Abiding strictly by the speed limit occurs when the knob is cranked up to the top numbers like say 9 and 10.

You turn the knob down to a 5 and tell the AI that you need to rush to work, even if it means going over the speed limit, which at a score of 5 it means that the AI driving system will mildly exceed the speed limit, though not in places like school zones, and only when the traffic situation seems to allow for safely going faster than the speed limit by a smidgeon.

The AI self-driving car gets you to work on-time!

Later that night, when heading home, you are not in as much of a rush, so you put the knob back to the 9 or 10 that it earlier was set at.

Also, you have a child-lock on the knob, such that when your kids use the self-driving car, which they can do on their own since there isn't a human driver needed, the knob is always set at the topmost of the scale and the children cannot alter it.

How does that seem to you?

Some self-driving car pundits find the concept of such a tuning knob to be repugnant.

They point out that everyone will "cheat" and put the knob on the lower scores that will allow the AI to do the same kind of shoddy and dangerous driving that humans do today. Whatever we might have otherwise gained by having self-driving cars, such as the hoped-for reduction in car crashes, along with the reduction in associated injuries and fatalities, will be lost due to the tuning knob capability.

Others though point out that it is ridiculous to think that people will put up with self-driving cars that are restricted drivers that never bend or break the law.

You'll end-up with people opting to rarely use self-driving cars and will instead drive their human-driven cars. This is because they know that they can drive more fluidly and won't be stuck inside a self-driving car that drives like some scaredy-cat.

As you might imagine, the ethical ramifications of an ethics tuning knob are immense.

In this use case, there is a kind of obviousness about the impacts of what an ethics tuning knob foretells.

Other kinds of AI systems will have their semblance of what an ethics tuning knob might portend, and though it might not be as readily apparent as the case of self-driving cars, there is potentially as much at stake in some of those other AI systems too (which, like a self-driving car, might entail life-or-death repercussions).

Conclusion

If you really want to get someone going about the ethics tuning knob topic, bring up the allied matter of the Trolley Problem.

The Trolley Problem is a famous thought experiment involving having to make choices about saving lives and which path you might choose. This has been repeatedly brought up in the context of self-driving cars and garnered acrimonious attention along with rather diametrically opposing views on whether it is relevant or not.

In any case, the big overarching questions are will we expect AI to have an ethics tuning knob, and if so, what will it do and how will it be used.

Those that insist there is no cause to have any such device are apt to equally insist that we must have AI that is only and always at the upmost of ethical behavior.

Is that a Utopian perspective or can it be achieved in the real world as we know it?

Only my crystal ball can say for sure.

CHAPTER 10

MIGHTY DUST STORM
AND
AI SELF-DRIVING CARS

CHAPTER 10

MIGHTY DUST STORM

AND

AI SELF-DRIVING CARS

Meteorologists are closely following some mega-sized dust plumes that are slowly drifting from the Sahara Desert and for which those murky clouds have already descended upon the normally scenic Caribbean islands, causing tourists and locals alike to find themselves immersed in the air stifling stuff.

Recent pictures were taken of the usual blue skies and wide ocean expanses at islands such as St. Barth's and Antigua and vividly showcased a nasty blanket of dust as far as the eye can see. Forget about those breathtaking ocean views and instead hold your breath to keep from inhaling the swath of gagging dust particles.

In Barbados, a severe dust haze warning was raised by authorities and urged special caution for those with respiratory difficulties, beseeching them to stay inside and protect themselves from the unseemly muck.

The unwelcome dust is already edging toward southern Florida, aiming soon to relentlessly spread throughout Texas and much of the southeastern United States.

Some that live in those regions are already accustomed to the Saharan Air Layer (SAL) oozing over to the U.S. on an annual basis and particularly during the summer months. You can place the blame on either favorable or unfavorable Trade Winds that bring this dusty invasion to our shores.

Beware the invasion of the creeping dust.

The good news, if you want a happy face version of the dustup, will be a lot of quite colorful sunrises and sunsets. This is due to how the dust and the light of the sun interact in the atmosphere, often creating some of the most eye-catching and snapshot worthy moments of the year.

It is hard to find much other joy in the majestic dust balls.

Sure, you might rejoice in the scientific theory that there are crucial nutrients embedded in the Saharan launched soil, and by being brought over via the prevailing winds this unexpected nourishment enriches the coral reefs off of Florida and the Bahamas.

That's something nice.

On the other hand, other scientists argue that this same dust is just as likely to harm the coral reefs, possibly shedding contaminants from the agriculturally treated desert soil and that even the untainted earthen materials might be over-fertilizing the coral waters to produce ungainly and unwanted algae blooms.

Seems like vast plumes of dust are a hard phenomenon to relish.

Well, there is a big reason to hope for massive dust clouds, namely they are known for being hurricane wreckers.

The thick dust in the air seems to cut down on the number and potency of hurricanes. The stark aridness brought by the dust is known to undermine the development and accumulation of moisture that is needed as a precept for hurricane formulations. Without the wetness, there are typically fewer hurricanes and they are less ferocious than might otherwise be the case.

Which would you choose, tons of dust swirling in the air and surrounding you like an unsightly blanket (minus hurricanes), or having perfectly clear skies that are then accompanied by horrendous hurricanes?

I suppose you prefer clear skies *and* no hurricanes, though that does not seem to be an available option, sorry to say.

In any case, there is definitely a lot of talk about this latest dust plume and the International Space Station is likewise keeping tabs on the enormous cloud, including issuing tweets by on-board astronauts as they marvel at the magnitude of this particular dust ball flare-up.

Regrettably, get ready to shelter in place again for those of you that have already been doing so, just as you thought it might be feasible to venture back outside.

Besides the obvious health consequences of these dust storms, there are other repercussions too.

Have you ever driven your car in a dust storm?

If not, you are lucky to have avoided the agony and abject fear that goes along with trying to drive in thick layers of flying soil.

Your visibility is cut way down.

Pedestrians seem to abruptly appear out of nowhere, and you are often suddenly at the rear bumper of the car ahead of you, doing so without any visible realization beforehand.

Attempts to use your windshield wipers are not effective and you quickly drain the windshield wiper fluid stored in the engine compartment tank.

In addition to the driving difficulties, your car doesn't like dust either.

An engine can potentially seize-up if the dust were to get fully under-the-hood, plus the odds are that you are going to have to do some maintenance shortly after any lengthy dust driving journeys.

As for the paint on the car, might as well start looking to see if Al's paint-and-body shop is going to be open for business since you will be needing a touch-up or two.

Anyway, if the car can withstand the dust difficulties, the mainstay of concern is that anyone driving in dust storms is heightening their risk of getting into a car crash. Car crashes invariably are accompanied by concomitant injuries and fatalities.

People are supposed to drive slowly and cautiously in dust storms.

Oddly, ironically perhaps, it seems that a segment of drivers believes in doing just the opposite. They seem to think that if you drive faster, you are better off. Presumably, their logic is that you will get through the dust storm in less time and therefore have less overall roadway threat exposures. This might appear to be compelling logic, but it is without sufficient merit and you ought to slow down and be driving carefully, or preferably not get on the road at all during a dust storm.

I'm sure that some that have driven quickly and survived many dust storms while driving at rocket-like speeds are going to carp and claim they are living proof that going faster is a sound approach. My sympathies to those that encounter these "free spirit" drivers and I can only hope that whatever miracle has been aiding them so far will continue during their continued and crazed driving sprints.

Speaking of driving, we might eventually see the day that there are either no human drivers or certainly a less-so number of human drivers on the highways and byways, coming about due to the advent of self-driving cars.

You might be wondering how self-driving cars might fare when faced with dust storms.

That brings up this interesting question: *Will AI-based true self-driving cars be able to cope with dust storms and how will they perform in contrast to human-driven cars?*

Let's unpack the matter and see.

Understanding The Levels Of Self-Driving Cars

As a clarification, true self-driving cars are ones that the AI drives the car entirely on its own and there isn't any human assistance during the driving task.

These driverless vehicles are considered a Level 4 and Level 5 while a car that requires a human driver to co-share the driving effort is usually considered at a Level 2 or Level 3. The cars that co-share the driving task are described as being semi-autonomous, and typically contain a variety of automated add-on's that are referred to as ADAS (Advanced Driver-Assistance Systems).

There is not yet a true self-driving car at Level 5, which we don't yet even know if this will be possible to achieve, and nor how long it will take to get there.

Meanwhile, the Level 4 efforts are gradually trying to get some traction by undergoing very narrow and selective public roadway trials, though there is controversy over whether this testing should be allowed per se.

Since semi-autonomous cars require a human driver, the adoption of those types of cars won't be markedly different than driving conventional vehicles, so there's not much new per se to cover about them on this topic (though, as you'll see in a moment, the points next made are generally applicable).

For semi-autonomous cars, it is important that the public needs to be forewarned about a disturbing aspect that's been arising lately, namely that despite those human drivers that keep posting videos of themselves falling asleep at the wheel of a Level 2 or Level 3 car, we all need to avoid being misled into believing that the driver can take away their attention from the driving task while driving a semi-autonomous car.

You are the responsible party for the driving actions of the vehicle, regardless of how much automation might be tossed into a Level 2 or Level 3.

Self-Driving Cars And Dealing With Dust Storms

For Level 4 and Level 5 true self-driving vehicles, there won't be a human driver involved in the driving task.

All occupants will be passengers.

The AI is doing the driving.

In terms of dust storms, do not falsely assume that the AI is going to be foolproof and always be able to drive in the thick muck of swirling soil.

This is worth mentioning because some recent polls and surveys seem to suggest that the public's understanding of self-driving cars is that the AI can drive the vehicle anywhere and everywhere, regardless of the circumstances or surroundings.

Keep in mind that part of the core principles about AI self-driving cars is that they are intended to be able to drive in the same realms that humans can drive. If a proficient human driver was unable to drive in a given setting, there is no expectation that an AI self-driving car can otherwise do so.

Note that this doesn't mean that it isn't still possible for the AI self-driving car to drive in those instances, but it is not considered a "requirement" per se that it is supposed to be able to do so. Also, people are often shocked to discover that the AI standardized driving levels do not include off-road driving within their scope, as such, there is no requirement or obligation for an AI self-driving car to be able to drive in off-road settings.

One pet peeve that I have repeatedly pressed too is the tendency for some to inappropriately refer to AI driving systems as being "superhuman" and for which this is decidedly misleading and outright a dangerous impression to create (including Elon Musk referring to Tesla's Autopilot as so-called superhuman).

At this time, AI driving systems are less capable than humans in various ways, and in other ways potentially better, but they are not altogether above and beyond human driving.

We have a long way to go on that goal.

Okay, so the first point is that we should not and cannot expect that AI self-driving cars will necessarily be able to drive in dust storms.

You might be puzzled that they would ever be unable to do so, since they are jampacked with state-of-the-art sensors including specialized cameras, radar, LIDAR, thermal imaging, ultrasonic units, and so on.

With all that high-tech gear it would seem they must be able to deal with dust in the air.

Sorry, the dust can be just as beguiling to the AI as it is to us, humans.

You might be aware that Waymo is testing their self-driving cars in Phoenix, Arizona, which is a desert-based area that from time-to-time has dust storms. When dust storms become large enough, scientists refer to those sizable dust storms as a haboob. The Phoenix valley has seen some doozie of haboob's, sometimes reaching up to several thousand feet high and roaming across hundreds of square miles.

For a short video of a Waymo self-driving vehicle in an Arizona dust storm..

Here's what happens when a self-driving car tries to undertake driving in a severe dust storm.

First, the camera is going to be less capable of detecting the roadway scene due to the confluence of dust particles in the air. This obscuring of the visual aspects of driving is about the same as when a human is driving a car, namely, it is darned hard to see what is out and about.

You could try to argue that the cameras are solely intended to capture visual images and video, and not prone to distraction as a human might be when eyeing their surroundings, and thus the cameras are a better bet than a human with their eyeballs.

Also, presumably, the AI is not struck by any fear about the driving task, which a human might become consumed with and therefore be less attentive to the road and more likely to make a driving mistake in a terrifying situation.

Yes, those are reasons to vote for the cameras as handy for dealing with a dust storm.

On the other hand, those cameras have lenses, and if the lenses get scratched or marred by the darting dust, you suddenly have a camera that no longer has a fully viable image to make use of. The camera could become entirely blotted by a smush of dirt and dust, becoming essentially blind to the road around it.

A human driver is presumably inside a car and less likely to get dust into their eyes, though certainly if they open a side window to try and look outside the vehicle or otherwise allow the dust to get in, you have a chance that the human driver might get muck in their eyes too. Recall too that the windshield can be difficult to keep clear.

In any case, by visual means alone, neither the AI and nor a human can see as far ahead, they cannot see what might be hidden at the side of the road, they might not realize a pedestrian is walking across the road or about to enter into the road, and so on.

Prudently, the AI is usually programmed to slow down and drive cautiously in any setting whereby the cameras are being visually constrained.

Of course, most self-driving cars are already crafted to drive gingerly, to begin with (such as not going above the speed limit and coming to complete stops and not do rolling stops, etc.), but they might sometimes include added provisions for special circumstances such as dust storms, heavy fog, and other weather situations.

This brings up another essential aspect of self-driving cars, consisting of their ODD (Operational Design Domain).

In the case of Level 4 self-driving cars, an automaker or self-driving tech firm is supposed to define an ODD that delineates the situations that are suitable for their AI driving system to be utilized.

For example, an ODD might be that the AI driving system is intended to properly operate during daylight and in non-rainy conditions. If it begins to rain, the AI is supposed to detect this facet and then realize that its ODD is being exceeded, in which case it should safely come to a halt and wait until the ODD conditions revert into its scope.

The main effort by most of the existing self-driving car entities is to establish and deploy their vehicles in rather everyday conditions and then deal with extraordinary conditions later on, once they have sufficiently dealt with the day-to-day driving tasks.

This is worthwhile mentioning since a dust storm would be most likely considered outside the ODD of today's self-driving cars, considered an outlier weather condition that is not a high priority right now, sometimes referred to as an edge or corner case.

All told, this means that if you were in a self-driving car during a dust storm, the odds are that the AI was not yet crafted to cope with the dust storm from a driving perspective, and thus it would rather quickly alert that it was going to safely pull over and wait out the conditions.

We might expect human drivers to do the same.

In other words, do not try driving in a bad dust storm and instead find a safe place to park and wait out the conditions.

Furthermore, we would likely advise to not even start a driving journey if it is known or likely that a dust storm is going to be occurring somewhere during your driving journey. Don't get on the road until the roadway conditions are amenable to safe driving.

Recall that earlier I mentioned that self-driving cars are usually loaded with a bunch of different kinds of sensors.

In theory, if the cameras are obscured or having difficulties, the AI can be using the other sensors to try and make up for the visual impairments.

The whole notion of MSDF (Multi-Sensor Data Fusion) is that the AI can bring together disparate data from different types of sensors, arrayed around the perimeter of the car, and fuse the collected data to try and arrive at a comprehensive and timely indication of what is taking place outside of the vehicle.

Despite that holistic approach, realize that in a rowdy dust storm the radar and LIDAR are likely to also have difficulties in sensing what is going on, partially due to the multitude of floating particles that can cause all sorts of added noise, misdirected reflections, and cause other problematic issues.

Thus, though having a variety of sensory types is an advantage, it does not guarantee that a dust storm can be dealt with.

Conclusion

Would you like a mind-bender?

There are AI Ethics related considerations that arise in these kinds of driving situations.

You are needing to get to the doctor's office urgently and would normally get into your car and hurriedly drive there.

Suppose the only cars available are self-driving cars.

So, you summon a self-driving car and get in, telling the AI via its Natural Language Processing (NLP) the address of your doctor.

The AI calculates that there is a dust storm in that area and refuses to drive.

The AI is being thoughtful about your safety and does not want to get mired in a dust storm while on the road and possibly get into a car accident that could get you harmed.

On the other hand, you have your reasons for wanting to take a chance and get to the doctor.

Should you be able to override the AI and insist that it drive you, or are you stuck until the AI declares that it is safe to go?

There are plenty of these kinds of AI ethics scenarios that are not yet resolved and we won't especially encounter them until there is a wider prevalence of self-driving cars.

Meanwhile, for those of you in the southeastern region of the U.S. that are going to be engulfed with dust, you might just find yourself facing a similar ethical dilemma as might an AI driving system, requiring you to gauge whether driving or not driving is the proper choice when a dust storm is enveloping you.

Good luck, stay out of the dust, and drive safely!

CHAPTER 11

AMAZON BUYS ZOOX AND AI SELF-DRIVING CARS

CHAPTER 11

AMAZON BUYS ZOOX
AND
AI SELF-DRIVING CARS

It is time to blare the trumpets and roll out the red carpet for some good old-fashioned sayings that explain the recent announcement of mighty Amazon buying comparatively teensy tiny Zoox, a notable self-driving car maker known primarily to Autonomous Vehicle (AV) insiders.

Try these sayings on for size:
- Great minds think alike
- Imitation is the highest form of flattery
- If you want to beat them, join them

Well, admittedly that last quip is not quite in its traditional form but fits indubitably to the situation.

Here's the behind the scenes shenanigans and posturing.

After the Amazon and Zoox announcement, Elon Musk sent out a tweet aimed at Jeff Bezos that ribbed him for being a copycat, presumably of Tesla (flavorfully, the tweet used a cat emoji, adding more spice to the tease).

In short, the bantering is that by Bezos buying Zoox via Amazon, the humongous e-commerce firm is going to become a head-to-head competitor with Tesla's self-driving ambitions.

You could view this as two titans that are now going to be fiercely locked in hand-to-hand combat (note that Amazon had already been dabbling in the self-driving industry, but one could say that this purchase of Zoox is a bold and gauntlet tossing stance).

That is why Musk can taunt Bezos as being an imitator or copycat, kind of like hey-dude, welcome to the party, finally.

One interpretation of this move by Bezos is that it showcases a staunch belief that self-driving cars are going to be vital and therefore are worthy of making a sizable investment (reportedly, Amazon is paying around $1.2B for Zoox, which seems hefty, but is loose change for Amazon some would say).

On the other hand, given that Zoox was previously reportedly valued at around $3B or more, some wring their hands that this rock bottom price for a self-driving firm reveals the softness in this space and stokes anew qualms that self-driving might not happen, or at least not happen for a long time to come.

The counterargument is that achieving self-driving is a money-hungry game and trying to get customary investors to pitch-in for a future that might be rosy and yet far off on the horizon, and maybe not even attainable, makes it incredibly difficult to remain as a standalone AV developer.

You need to have deep pockets and a willingness to have dogged patience to make it in this niche, of which Amazon potentially has those kinds of traits.

Sure, you could say that Amazon likely got an enormously discounted price, partially as a result of the recent pullbacks by all self-driving efforts in light of societal and economic conditions, but it allows Zoox to keep pushing forward and seemingly prevents what would be a hurtful loss to this industry if Zoox could not find some other attractive means to get new financing.

There is more to this story though than meets the obvious eye.

Allow me a moment to bring you up-to-speed.

What Does Self-Driving Mean

As background, Zoox is a self-driving car maker based in Silicon Valley that started in 2014 and has been an upstart ever since. What makes them outside the norm is their profound and unshakable belief that self-driving cars need to be derived from the ground up.

What does that mean?

Many of the self-driving software development entities are aiming their autonomous capabilities at conventional cars that are supplemented with elaborate sensor suites and other augmentations to render them into autonomously driven vehicles.

Meanwhile, though Zoox has been doing the same by making use of specially outfitted Toyota Highlanders and Prius C's, their overarching passion is to entirely reinvent the car as a platform.

For example, in a human-driven car, it makes sense to always architect a car to drive forwards, since the human is sitting in a fixed position facing forward. That is the way we've sat and driven cars throughout the modern history of this amazing invention.

But in a self-driving car, the AI is doing the driving, and as such you could engineer the vehicle to readily drive forward in either direction.

Thus, scratch the archaic notion of at times driving "backward" and instead flip the driver orientation to being forwards, always, even if you perchance happen to be going in the reverse direction of which you just came.

They refer to this as a symmetrical and bidirectional design, plus the vehicle would be a zero-emissions Electrical Vehicle (EV).

You might be wondering, which is the better route to go, namely whether to add complex space-age stuff onto conventional cars or reimagine anew what a car consists of.

The rub is that if you decide to go the seemingly radical route and attempt a never-been-done-before design, you potentially have two major battles to confront simultaneously.

You have to ensure that the physical car itself can work and be safe on the roads and at the same time you also have to make sure that the AI and the self-driving stuff works properly too. That is why many of the self-driving car related efforts are focused on using various augmented everyday cars, attempting to reduce the variability and uncertainties in what is otherwise inarguably a moonshot-like aspiration.

The logic is that you might prudently ease into the self-driving car realm by having a rock-solid foundation based on an already proven car, and thus deal only with the angst and throes underpinning the AI self-driving capabilities.

Zoox is essentially trying to have its cake and eat it too, doing so by using selected models of conventional cars that have been augmented with self-driving tech, including putting those onto the roadways for real-world tryouts, and pushing with great zeal behind-the-scenes on formulating a brand new purpose-built kind of car.

If you have followed me so far on this explanation, let's next dig more deeply into considering the multi-dimensional mind-bending implications of the tweet from Elon Musk.

Everybody knows that Musk has been aiming to have Tesla become not just a premier automaker but also be the preeminent self-driving car provider too. Via the use of Autopilot and the sensors packaged into a Tesla vehicle, step-by-step there has been an incremental effort to gradually transform the semi-autonomous driving into a fully autonomous driving vehicle.

Let's make sure that everyone reading this knows one very clear cut and irrefutable point: ***Today's Tesla's are not fully autonomous.***

Despite whatever wild claims you hear, and those idiotic videos online of people falsely believing their Tesla can drive itself, this is a complete crock and a regrettable and dangerous falsehood. With today's Tesla's and all their "autopiloting" features, it is still a car that requires a human driver. On the autonomous driving scale, you would say that the vehicles are a Level 2.

True autonomous cars are at a Level 4 and someday at a hoped-for Level 5.

Zoox is focusing on Level 4 and Level 5.

Tesla is at a Level 2 and trying to progressively make its way to a Level 4 and Level 5.

So you could readily indicate that both Tesla and Zoox are ultimately seeking to achieve true self-driving, though Tesla is doing so from a lesser level of semi-autonomous driving, while Zoox is skipping past those lower levels and striving instead for the topmost ones.

Nobody can say for sure which path is the better route.

Firms like Tesla would undoubtedly claim they are taking the "right" approach by a stepwise refinement methodology.

What many people do not quite seem to realize is that Tesla is opening themselves to a lot of costly risks and potential downfall by embarking upon Level 2 and presumably into a Level 3.

I've exhorted repeatedly that we are going to have human drivers that do not take seriously their responsibilities as the driver of a Level 2 or Level 3 car.

When there are car crashes involving Level 2 and Level 3 vehicles, the automaker immediately attempts to absolve themselves of all blame by pointing out that the human driver is the responsible party for the driving task. Whether this will continue to grant those firms a kind of scot-free liability remains to be seen, and my prediction is that there will likely be massive lawsuits that are going to potentially severely ding such firms and even put some of them out-of-business.

As such, some maintain that the path of Zoox and others that are leapfrogging to Level 4 and eventually Level 5 is the more prudent approach, avoiding what might become an ugly and firm-destroying tussle by being mired in the muck of Level 2 and Level 3.

Of course, those in the Level 2 and Level 3 are apt to claim that it is more likely they will get to Level 4 and then Level 5, sooner, since they will have built their way there, learning and reusing as they go. And, meanwhile, they can rake in revenue from Level 2 and Level 3, versus those having essentially no revenue at all while struggling with getting Level 4 ready for use in the everyday world.

The additional twist is that some of the Level 4 and Level 5 aimers are using their autonomous driving capabilities for aspects other than solely driving a passenger-based car. By leveraging related use cases, this can potentially imbue those firms into viable revenue streams sooner and keep the lights on.

There are efforts of using self-driving delivery vehicles and other modes of transport such as autonomous shuttles that might be considered more readily viable, meanwhile potentially continuing the scuffles of problematic passenger car requirements (some believe that Amazon is most likely eyeing the use of Zoox capabilities for handling delivery and logistics mobility matters, more so than as rider or ride-sharing vehicle provider).

What Will Amazon Do With Zoox

In the case of Tesla, it seems rather apparent that Musk has a (heavy) hands-on approach and appears to be routinely if not daily putting his two cents into what is happening with Autopilot and the self-driving aspirations of the firm.

You would be hard-pressed to suggest that Musk does otherwise.

And probably get a tweet or two to set you straight.

What will happen with Zoox and the potential hands-on or maybe arms-length reach of Jeff Bezos?

According to the formal press release issued about the Amazon and Zoox deal, apparently, Zoox will remain as an independent operation within the Amazon empire.

Some are dubious about such a declaration, and we have seen similar such assertions made when a large firm buys another company and yet the independence radiance does not last for very long (if it ever even had a semblance of happening).

Put on your clairvoyance cap and let's examine the self-driving era crystal ball to see what might happen to Zoox while within Amazon.

Here are the Top Five scenarios:

- **Zoox Goes On Steroids** – in this scenario, Amazon internally pours a ton of dough into Zoox, finally allowing those AI developers and engineers to stop using duct tape and spit to keep things going, and the impact is steroid-enriched full steam ahead that catapults Zoox self-driving cars into becoming the topmost of the industry and advancing them at a lightning pace.

- **Zoox Tacks Due To Forceful Winds** – in this scenario, the take is that Amazon decides to stress-test the independence of Zoox by offering "suggestions" about what direction Zoox should be going, perhaps nixing, for now, the proprietary vehicle notion and insisting that only the AI self-driving is what counts, pushing the firm toward using existing vehicles augmented for self-driving, or offering some similar life-draining energy out of the entity.

- **Zoox Absorbed By The Borg** – in this scenario, you might as well put into your keepsake box any Zoox imprinted keychains and T-shirts and save them as collector's items since Zoox is going to disappear, becoming wholly absorbed into the Amazon Borg, maybe sad or not, and it is quite uncertain what the final result would be.

- **Zoox Evaporates Into Nonexistence** – in this scenario, Amazon does not especially fund Zoox and lets it dangle on the vine, gradually the talent gets grabbed up by other firms having the requisite strident determination and support for self-driving ambitions, the Zoox that is leftover looks a lot like a variation of Pied Piper and astonishingly Richard Hendricks is assigned by Amazon to lead the entity.

- **Zoox Fantasyland Arises** – in this scenario, Amazon aids in Zoox flourishing, what happens next is a twist beyond the imagination of many, Zoox dominates in self-driving and ends-up bringing in more money than does Amazon, indeed the e-commerce of Amazon gets sluggish, Zoox is to the rescue as it climbs into the trillions of dollars due to self-driving, Bezos looks back at his acquisition of Zoox and offers thanks to his lucky stars.

Which of those scenarios will playout?

Time will tell.

Conclusion

One thing you can say about the self-driving car realm is that there is never a dull moment.

Something is always happening.

At times, the self-driving dream is touted by the media and everyone rushes to get a piece of the pie, while at other times the doom-and-gloom settles in and people wonder whatever happened about those self-driving cars that were going to be ubiquitously zipping around on all of our highways and byways.

Take a moment to contemplate what the future will bring in terms of this new shakeup.

Has Bezos just bought himself the deal of the century?

Will Musk rue the day that he ribbed Bezos about the Zoox acquisition and find himself staring enviously at "AmaZoox" or is it "ZooxAma" when their self-driving vehicles are doing donuts around Teslas?

Or will Amazon absentmindedly drift onto other matters, and the only remaining reference to Zoox occurs whenever a trivia question asks what was the name of those single-celled dinoflagellates that live in coral and jellyfish, for which the answer is Zooxanthellae but some might reminisce and exclaim the word Zoox instead. Those that are skeptical about the Amazon and Zoox being a match made in heaven are apt to predict that Tesla cars will soon be sporting bumper stickers that declare: "My Other Car Was Going To Be A Zoox, But It Got Lost Somewhere In The Amazon."

Fans of Zoox are decidedly more upbeat, and with a Spock-like recital are solemnly stating that Zoox shall live long and prosper. For the sake of self-driving cars, hopefully, the passion and verve underlying Zoox will continue to survive and thrive, and the era of true self-driving cars will fervidly see its day.

CHAPTER 12
TESLA WITH LIDAR AND AI SELF-DRIVING CARS

CHAPTER 12

TESLA WITH LIDAR
AND
AI SELF-DRIVING CARS

Adding to how much the world has become topsy-turvy, an actual and official Tesla car was recently spotted wearing LIDAR sensor technology while traveling on public roadways.

Heavens!

For those of you that don't know why this would be especially newsworthy, you need to be brought up-to-speed over the LIDAR uproar that has and continues to engulf the advent of self-driving cars.

Let's get the record straight on the foundations of this messy and bitter topic.

I will endeavor to first bring you up-to-speed on the overarching saga, and then we can consider ways to explain this unexpected and somewhat stupefying sighting of an official Tesla car that had LIDAR on it, which is akin to spotting Bigfoot or the Loch Ness Monster, or like crossing the streams in the movie *Ghostbusters*, etc.

It is either a watershed moment, an optical illusion, or maybe one of seven seemingly bona fide ways to explain the unusual and extraordinary phenomenon (which I'll walk you through).

What LIDAR Is All About

LIDAR refers to a technology that combines the use of light via lasers and the application of radar-like techniques (light + radar), and for which such tech has been around since the late 1950s and has been used in a wide variety of ways.

It is nothing new per se.

The use of LIDAR has been considered a cornerstone of autonomous systems such as self-driving cars.

By shooting out laser beams and gauging how long they take to return, it is possible to try and map out whatever surrounds the LIDAR device, getting a semblance of the distance to those detected objects and thus identifying where they are and potentially their size (plus, over time, the movement of those objects as a series of such sightings are recorded and compared).

Initially, LIDAR sensors were relatively expensive, costing hundreds of thousands of dollars, which meant that though they were great for use on experimental self-driving cars, trying to use that costly kind of tech for production cars would make those vehicles prohibitively expensive.

As with most tech, LIDAR inexorably has come way down on price. The LIDAR devices have also gotten a lot smaller and more adept, along with being less error-prone and able to withstand the rigors of being on cars that endure daily weathering and the grit and grime of the world.

Here's a key point: *Nearly all automakers and self-driving tech firms have adopted the use of LIDAR, other than Tesla and Elon Musk.*

Some consider Elon Musk to be the leader of an anti-LIDAR camp.

Why would anyone be arguing against the use of LIDAR?

In the past, the easiest argument was that LIDAR was too costly, it was too big, it was impractical and so though maybe handy for doing experimental work, it did not have the right stuff for real-world use.

You would be hard-pressed to use that same argument today, though some still try.

In any case, setting aside all of that, the other question that people tend to ponder is whether LIDAR is essential for self-driving or whether it can be considered optional.

In other words, if the LIDAR devices are the only means to ensure that a self-driving car can make its way through traffic and do so without hitting things, the costs and other factors do not seem quite so crucial and one ought to be putting LIDAR onto cars without hesitation.

That takes us into one of the now loudest debates, namely the rancorous contention that LIDAR is unnecessary as it can be completely otherwise handled by cameras.

Some believers contend that the use of cameras is sufficient and there is no need to use LIDAR.

In their viewpoint, adding LIDAR is therefore an unnecessary added cost and complexity, no matter how low the cost might be and no matter how improved the tech has become. Generally, if you are a person that believes in parsimonious systems and do not perceive LIDAR as essential, you would say that though LIDAR might be handy, it is not needed, and including it is foolishly bulking up for no good reason.

No one can yet prove beyond a shadow of a doubt that cameras can completely serve solely and in absence of having LIDAR too. Thus, it is relatively customary that self-driving cars are outfitted with both cameras and LIDAR devices, along with radar, ultrasonic, thermal imaging, and a slew of such detection sensors.

Not so with Tesla.

Elon Musk early on decided that LIDAR was not needed for Tesla cars. At first, he left open that he might someday be proven wrong on this judgment call, and then, later on, decided to harden his position and shifted into denigrating the need for LIDAR.

Eventually, Musk went so far as to suggest that others using LIDAR were outright foolish in their doing so and would ultimately regret having used LIDAR.

Your reaction to this is likely that Musk is a sharp person and seems to know a lot about physics and science stuff, so he must have a valid basis for making these assertions, and especially so since they seem to go against the grain of the rest of the self-driving field.

Does Musk see something that others do not?

Perhaps he has a vision that goes beyond the purview of others and, as per his other bets on things like universal space exploration and the boring of large tunnels, he decidedly travels on a different path than the norm.

One argument that he has voiced about being essentially anti-LIDAR is that humans drive cars and do not have lasers spewing out light beams from their heads. As such, if a human can drive a car with the use of their good old plain eyeballs, it just stands to reason that a camera is the only thing particularly needed to achieve the equivalent of human driving levels of performance.

The immediate counter-argument is that he has opted to use radar, and yet human drivers do not have radar built into their skulls, thus, based on his sense of elucidated logic, shouldn't he ditch the use of radar from all Tesla cars?

Besides, presumably self-driving cars are hopefully going to be better drivers than humans, avoiding the 40,000 annual car fatalities in the United States alone, and mitigating the approximate 1.2 million injuries due to car crashes, which perhaps could use the added help of LIDAR, rather than eschewing something that might make that last mile difference in life-or-death results.

Another explanation as to why his now intransigent posture on anti-LIDAR has become so entrenched is that he has painted himself into a corner.

How so?

During the evolution and rollout of Tesla cars, Musk and Tesla have insisted and touted that your Tesla car has all the hardware that it needs to be self-driving ready. Presumably, only the software is missing to get there, and the software can be downloaded at some future time of readiness via the on-board OTA (Over-The-Air) electronic communications capabilities.

And, keep in mind, the hardware on a Tesla does not include LIDAR.

This all means that if he and Tesla were to recant their anti-LIDAR position, they would be on-the-hook to seemingly go around and retrofit every Tesla car with LIDAR devices.

Let that soak in for a moment.

Can you imagine the exorbitant cost and logistics nightmare of trying to ensure that every Tesla car was retrofitted with LIDAR devices?

Impractical.

The company could not afford to do so.

But, meanwhile, this also opens up a gate that just might end-up biting Tesla in the end.

You've undoubtedly seen in the news about various Tesla car crashes from time-to-time for which Autopilot, the semi-automated driving features and for which are not at all full self-driving as yet, was engaged.

Some of those incidents are lawsuits now (and some have settled out-of-court).

One risk exposure for Tesla involves the possibility that by not having included LIDAR, they might have chosen imprudently the safety of their cars. If the safety question was based on the cost of LIDAR, they essentially are calculating somehow that lives lost translates into some amount of dollars saved, so goes the argument, and it's the same kind of argument that undermined the famous Pinto car and other similar automotive design choices.

In all of that potential legal liability, some argue there will eventually be a day of reckoning for Tesla and Musk, whereby a court might decide that the firm owes big time for having made the anti-LIDAR decision and not backing down from it.

In that case, all of the sales of Tesla, impressive as they are, could be construed as merely bankrolling a future legal whopper of a case that goes against Tesla and imposes an astronomical financial penalty that could potentially wipe the company out.

That is the painted-into-a-corner scenario, wherein over time the firm has made its bed and has to lie in it, though the clock might be ticking, unbeknownst to most, and at some future point, an enormous price will need to be paid.

Furthermore, the fact that nearly all other self-driving cars have LIDAR is presumably going to be weighted as an indicator that Tesla knowingly and overtly decided how it wanted to proceed, undercutting any viable chance of claiming they did not know or comprehend the potential value of LIDAR.

All of that being said, the muddiness about LIDAR versus not using LIDAR could potentially serve as a type of protective cover for Tesla and this doomsday-like scenario might never play out.

What a story!

Welcome to the world of self-driving cars and the enduring and unresolved LIDAR-related debate.

Official Tesla Car With LIDAR On The Roadway

You are firmly briefed and ready for the latest twist.

There was recent breaking news about a Tesla car that was photographed on the public roadways while adorned with LIDAR in a protruding manner, notably attached to an on-the-rooftop rig.

Perhaps it is now keenly evident why this sighting would spark such outsized interest.

As I earlier mentioned, it is akin to abruptly seeing Bigfoot, with your eyes wide open, and standing right there in the middle of the street.

Astounding!

From a LIDAR versus anti-LIDAR stance, this might be likened to seeing the crossing of matter and anti-matter atomic beams, out of which you cannot be sure what might happen, including the possibility that all of existence will suddenly implode.

The first response by some was that it was undoubtedly done by an individual owner of a Tesla, opting to add LIDAR in a hobbyist fashion to their prized Tesla vehicle.

Not so, say the reports, since the vehicle had official Tesla automaker plates.

Another guess was that it was similar to some vendors that have showcased adding LIDAR onto a Tesla to indicate how it might look, but that does not explain away the official Tesla automaker plates.

Another possibility voiced was that the photos are fakes, doctored to make a Tesla look like it has LIDAR on it.

Well, though that might be a possibility, the reporting seems valid and the photos look truthful, though there is always an outside chance of a DeepFake or equivalent, which appears to be highly unlikely in this case.

Okay, let's then assume that Tesla was an actual official Tesla car and it was on the public roadways, and it was sporting LIDAR units.

Here are seven solid reasons that this Bigfoot sighting might make sense:

- **Temporary use of LIDAR for camera ground-truth calibration** – in this scenario, the LIDAR is being used to aid in calibrating the cameras of the Tesla, perhaps due to trying out some new software for the cameras or possibly even a new set of cameras, all of which does though tend to support the facet that LIDAR does have value, though the anti-LIDAR camp would retort that the value is only superfluous and not a necessity and nothing about this temporary use proves otherwise.

- **Anticipatory tryout of LIDAR for the vaunted Cybertruck** – in this scenario, perhaps the revered Cybertruck is going to have LIDAR included; notably, the Tesla car has a seemingly to-large rack that might be construed as an exoskeleton used to mimic the bulky profile of the Cybertruck, and if LIDAR is going to be in the self-driving Cyberrtruck Autopilot package then it makes sense to go ahead and use an everyday Tesla car on the roadways versus the higher profile and newsworthy act of driving a Cybertruck around town. In terms of whether using LIDAR on the Cybertrucks would be an admission of the utility of LIDAR, presumably, the counterargument would be that for a large-sized vehicle it is warranted whereas for a traditional sized passenger car it is not.

- **Reconsidering using LIDAR on existing Tesla cars** – in this scenario, which seems wholly unlikely and nearly unthinkable, these are tryouts of LIDAR to reconsider retrofitting existing Tesla cars, though if you fervently and genuinely believe that to be the case then you maybe ought to look into buying swampland too.

- **Considering using LIDAR on future Tesla cars** – this is a slightly more plausible scenario than the preceding one (but not by much), namely that future Tesla cars might come with LIDAR, but if so it is certainly going to be difficult to explain this turn of events and could put the company into hot water with all those existing Tesla owners and ardent fans of Tesla, including providing fodder for any legal proceedings.

- **Being used to "prove" that LIDAR is not necessary for Tesla's** – the anti-LIDAR camp would certainly treasure this scenario, whereby Tesla is purposely trying out LIDAR to then establish ironclad proof that it does not especially add value and thus put to rest the feisty debates on the topic. Would they go to this trouble just for spite, or might it be to defend themselves in court, when or if that day comes?

- **Rogue project inside Tesla that got caught in the open** – you know how wild and crazy those engineers are at Tesla, they love to play with their toys and maybe they got their hands on some LIDAR units, meanwhile one of them had an idea to plop them onto a Tesla and see how it goes. Even though Musk seems like the type of leader that encourages freewheeling thinking, it would be doubtful that he would be pleased upon finding out via a tweet or social media that his team was doing this kind of shenanigans behind-his-back (alternatively, with his style, promotions might be suddenly awarded).

- **Because they want to play with our minds** – we can all readily agree that Tesla and Musk enjoy playing with our minds and having some fun, so perhaps this was a trick and those LIDAR units are painted hockey pucks, or possibly they are real LIDAR devices but the whole rig is a publicity stunt. Have we been played, and if so, should we be happy about it or irked?

Conclusion

Which of the seven are you leaning toward?

Maybe in the metaphysics world of Musk and his thinking outside the box, there are other reasons that none of us can yet fathom or divine.

Since Musk also likes to at times grandly philosophize, perhaps the sighting isn't real and only a dream that we are all caught up in.

Could be.

Anyway, make sure to keep your eyes open for more sightings, get plenty of sleep to be ready for what comes next, perhaps infusing thoughts of LIDAR into your nighttime slumber, assuming that we aren't already in that same dreamy mental state every day (Musk would indubitably know if we are.

CHAPTER 13
AUTOPILOT BK WHOPPER AND AI SELF-DRIVING CARS

CHAPTER 12

AUTOPILOT BK WHOPPER

AND

AI SELF-DRIVING CARS

What do AI, self-driving cars, Tesla, Autopilot, and hamburgers such as the infamous Burger King Whopper all have in common?

Well, a whopper of a story, of course.

A recent ad campaign by Burger King has this smarmy catchphrase: "Smart cars are smart enough to brake for a Whopper."

And, just to make sure that the ad comes with all the toppings, they also indicate "Artificial Intelligence knows what you crave."

Admittedly, it is yet another notable example of Burger King cleverly leveraging what otherwise might have been a smalltime viral social media item into something indubitably marketable to sell those vaunted burgers and fries. This time their eagle eye and caustic wit involve a facet of automation that powers self-driving cars and perchance involves the use of a Tesla running Autopilot, which is not yet a full-fledged self-driving capability.

Here's the backstory about the so-called Autopilot Whopper tale.

In May of this year, a video was posted on YouTube by a driver recording a highway driving journey that purports to showcase a Tesla running Autopilot that mistakenly classifies a roadside Burger King sign as possibly a stop sign.

Note that the car merely began to slow down, gradually, and did not react jerkily or opt to radically try to come to a halt upon detecting what it interpreted as a possible stop sign.

How do we know what the car was trying to do?

Per the video recording made by the driver, the console screen in the Tesla flashes the classic message of "Stopping for traffic control" that is a usual message to let the human driver know that the system detects some form of traffic condition warranting the car to be brought to a halt by the computer.

The car remained in motion on the highway, and once the distance to the roadside sign diminished, the alert about an upcoming traffic control no longer displayed and the vehicle accelerated back up to the posted speed limit.

You might say this was a no-harm, no-foul situation.

No one was hurt, no car crash ensued, and it does not appear that traffic was disturbed in the least.

That being said, yes, the automation did falsely at first interpret that the detected sign might be a stop sign and began to reduce speed accordingly, but once the car got close enough to make a more ascertained analysis, the system figured out that it was not a stop sign and continued unabated in traffic.

Let's take the video at face value and assume it is not faked or otherwise doctored.

I mention this caveat since someone could readily craft such a video via any decent video editing software, but generally, the video seems to be a likely indication of what happened and we can reasonably assume it is an actual occurrence.

Your first thought, perhaps similar to mine, consisted of whether this was a perchance one-time fluke or whether it would potentially happen a second time, a third time, and so on.

We do not know for sure if it was repeatable per se, though about a month or so later, the same driver drove the same way again and posted a newer video showing that the Tesla did not appear to make the same mistake.

In that subsequent video, the driver verbally congratulates Tesla for the seeming facet that the car had presumably "learned" to deal with the Burger King sign and no longer was falsely categorizing it as a stop sign.

We cannot necessarily make that leap of logic, nor leap of faith.

Why so?

There could be other plausible reasons for why the vehicle did not react the same way as it had done the first time.

Allow me a moment to elaborate.

Imagine when you are driving a car and sometimes you might see something as based on the lighting and other environmental conditions, and you see a sign in a sharper way or a more occluded manner, depending upon the amount of sunshine, cloud cover, and the like.

It could be that the camera detection differed from the first time and thus by luck of the draw the subsequent drive-by did not spot the sign at all, or it spotted the sign but got a better look at it this time.

Realize that at a distance, a camera picture or video is going to have less detail and be dealing with objects that are only vaguely visible. Again, this is somewhat like how you might strain to figure out a faraway object, and similarly, the on-board computer system attempts to classify whatever it can see, even if only seen faintly.

Many that are not involved in self-driving tech do not realize that driving, even by humans, consists of a game of probabilities and uncertainties.

When you see something up ahead on the road resembling say roadway debris, a stationary object that is sitting on the road, you might not know if it is a hard object akin to a dropped toolbox from the bed of a truck, or maybe it is an empty cardboard box and relatively harmless.

Until you get closer, you are pondering what the object might be, along with trying to decide in advance as to what course of action you should take. If you can switch lanes, maybe you should do so to avoid hitting the object. If you cannot readily switch lanes, maybe it is better to try and roll over the top of the object and thus not take other extreme measures like swerving or screeching to a halt.

This brings up an important lesson about AI and self-driving tech, which is that it is not going to operate in some magical way and drive in pure perfection. Just as a human will struggle to identify what a roadway piece of debris is, and has to ascertain driving options, likewise the AI has to do the same.

That's also why I keep exhorting that this notion of zero fatalities due to adopting AI driving systems is a false set of expectations.

We are still going to have car crashes, despite having AI driving systems. In some cases, it could be that the AI "judges" improperly and takes the wrong driving action, while in other situations such as a pedestrian that unexpectedly darts in front of a moving car there are no viable alternatives available to avoid a collision.

Keep in mind that even the revered AI-based true self-driving car is still bound by the law of physics.

When something untoward happens, suddenly, without apparent prewarning, you can only stop a car as based on physics and cannot miraculously cause the vehicle to instantaneously cease in motion. Stopping distances are still stopping distances, regardless of human-driven versus AI-driven cars.

That being said, it is certainly hoped that by having AI driving systems that fully operate a car, the number of car crashes due to human drunk driving and various human driving foibles will be significantly reduced and we will have a lot less injury and fatalities on our roadways (but, I emphasize, still not zero).

In any case, just because the car did not repeat the mistaken identification of the Burger King sign on the subsequent run, we cannot assume that it was due to the car "learning" about the matter.

Unless we are allowed to dig into the Autopilot system and the data being collected, it is not readily determinable what has perhaps altered, though it does seem like a reasonable guess that the system might have changed and can do a better job on dealing with the Burger King sign.

What Is This Thing Learning

Let's suppose it was the case that the system was better able to categorize the Burger King sign.

Does that mean that the system "learned" about the matter?

First, whenever you use the word "learn" it can overstate what a piece of automation is doing. In a sense, the use of this moniker is what some people refer to as anthropomorphizing the automation.

Here's why.

Suppose that AI developers and engineers in the backroom were examining the data being collected by their cars, including the video streams, and realized that the Burger King sign was being falsely classified as a stop sign. Those human developers might have tweaked the system to prevent it from doing so again.

In that case, would you describe the automation as having "learned" what to do?

Seems like a stretch.

Or, suppose that the system was using Machine Learning (ML) or Deep Learning (DL), consisting of an Artificial Neural Network (ANN), which is a type of mathematical pattern matching approach that tries to somewhat mimic how the human brain might work (please be aware that today's computer-based neural networks are a far cry from how the brain works, not at all equivalent, and generally a night and day kind of difference of the real thing).

It could be that the HQ computer system on the backend via data collected from cars in the fleet has assembled the data into a cloud database, and might be set up to examine false positives (a false positive is when the detection algorithm thinks there is something there such as a stop sign, but it is not a stop sign).

Upon computationally discovering the Burger King as a false positive, the system mathematically might flag that any such an image is decidedly not a stop sign and then this flag is pushed out to the cars in the fleet, doing so via the OTA (Over-The-Air) electronic communications that allow HQ to send data and program patches to the vehicles.

Could you describe this as "learning" about Burger King signs?

Well, you might try to make such a claim, exploiting the aspect that the computational methods are known as Machine Learning and Deep Learning, but for some this a stretch of the meaning associated with learning in any human-like manner.

For example, a human that learned to not mistake Burger King signs might also have learned a lot of other facets at the same time. A human might generalize and realize that McDonald's signs could be misinterpreted, maybe Taco Bell signs, and so on, all of which are part of the overarching semblance of learning.

You could take that further.

A human might learn about the whole concept that sometimes there are signs that resemble something else that we know, and thus, it is vital to carefully not assume that the traits of the Burger King sign are carried over into other aspects of making false identifications.

This might also prompt the human to think about how they make other false assumptions based on quick judgments. Whenever they see someone, from a distance, perhaps judging them as to whether they are a certain kind of person is a premature act.

And so on.

I realize you might be pained to contemplate how far a human would really take the instance of a misclassified Burger King sign, but that misses the point I am trying to make.

My point is that when a human learns, they usually (or hopefully) generalize that learning in a multitude of other ways. Some lump this into the idea that we have common sense and can perform common-sense reasoning.

Shocker for you: *There is not yet any AI that has any bona fide semblance of common-sense reasoning.*

Some assert that until we can get AI to embody common-sense reasoning, we will not achieve true AI, the kind of AI that is the equivalent of human intelligence, which nowadays is referred to as AGI or Artificial General Intelligence (suggesting that today's typical AI is much narrower and simpler in scope and capability than the aspired version of AI).

Overall, you would be hard-pressed to say that car automation has "learned" from the Burger King incident in any generalizable and full-reasoning way that a human might.

In any case, people like to use the word "learn" when referring to today's variant of AI, though it overstates what is happening and can cause overinflated and confounding expectations.

The Puzzle About The Sign

You might remember the famous scene in the movie *Princess Bride* involving a battle of wits, and one of the characters brazenly touts that he has only begun to proffer his logic.

Let's use that same bravado here.

We have so far assumed that the Burger King sign was classified as a stop sign, momentarily so, while the car was traveling on a highway and approaching the off-highway signage.

You might be thinking, why in the heck is a sign that isn't actually on the roadway being examined as a potential stop sign and being given due consideration for coming to a stop?

When driving your car on the highway, there are dozens upon dozens of off-highway stop signs and a slew of other traffic control signs that are quite readily visible from the highway, and yet you do not deem them worthy of bringing your car to a halt while on the highway.

This is because you know that those signs are off the roadway and have nothing to do with your driving whilst on the highway.

Imagine if every time you saw a formal traffic sign for local streets and yet they were not on the highway that you opted to react as though they were positioned on the highway.

What a mess!

You would be continually doing all sorts of crazy driving antics on the highway and be confusing all the other nearby drivers.

In short, since the Burger King sign was not on the highway, it should have instantly been disregarded as a traffic control sign or any kind of sign worthy of attention by the automation. We could go extreme and say that if the Burger King sign was identical to a stop sign, in essence, replace the Burger King logo with an actual stop sign, this still should not matter.

This brings us back to the so-called "learning" aspects.

If the automation now has a computational indication that a Burger King sign is not a stop sign, this seems insufficient. We would also want it to "learn" that signs off the highway are not relevant to the highway driving, though, of course, there are exceptions that make this a necessarily flexible rule and you cannot simply declare that all off-the-road signs can be completely disregarded.

Why did the automation seem to initially assess that the Burger King sign pertained to the highway?

There is a bit of an optical trick involved and one that typically impacts human drivers too.

The Burger King sign was atop a tall pole and standing relatively close to the highway.

If you have ever seen their prominent signs, they are notable because they have "Burger King" spelled out in bright red letters, boldly proclaimed, and the shape of the sign is an oval, all of which does resemble from a distance the same overall look of a stop sign. Of course, the sign is purposely facing the highway to attract maximum attention.

In this driving scenario, the car comes over a crest in the highway and the Burger King sign appears to be immediately adjacent to the highway and possibly could be construed as on the highway itself, as seen from a distance and based on the highway structure and coming over the crest.

You most certainly have experienced such visual illusions before, and it is an easy phenomenon to fall for.

Once you realize it is a Burger King sign, you don't care anymore whether it is on the highway or off the highway since it does not require any action on your part (well, unless you are hungry and the signage sparks you to get off the highway for a burger).

In theory, a human driver could have done the same thing that the automation did, namely begin to slow down as a precautionary act in case the sign was a stop sign. A novice driver might especially get caught by this kind of visual illusion the first few times they experience it, and thereafter presumably get the gist of what they are seeing.

In that sense, as a human, you are learning by experience, essentially collecting data and then adjusting based on the data that you've collected.

Potentially, the Machine Learning or Deep Learning that the automaker has established for self-driving automation can do somewhat likewise.

A training data set is usually put together to try and train the ML/DL on what kinds of roadway signs to expect. The training data must include a sufficient variety of examples, otherwise, the computational calculations will overfit to the data and only those signs that are strictly obedient to the true sign will be later detectable.

In the real world, stop signs are oftentimes defaced, bashed, or bent, possibly partially covered by tree limbs, and all sorts of other variations exist.

If you used only the cleanest of stop signs to do the training of the ML/DL, the resultant in-car detection would undoubtedly be unable to ascertain lots of everyday and real-world distressed stop signs that are posted.

One of the nightmare dangers for any self-driving car is the possibility of false negatives.

A false negative is when let's say a stop sign exists, but the automation does not construe the stop sign as a stop sign.

This is bad.

The automation could fail to make a required stop and the cataclysmic result could be a car crash and horrific outcomes.

You could also assert somewhat the same about false positives. Suppose the automation fully mistook the Burger King sign as a stop sign and did come to a halt on the highway. Other drivers behind the stopped car could readily ram into the car since it inexplicably and unexpectedly stopped in the middle of a normally rushing along the highway.

Conclusion

Welcome to the conundrum facing those that are crafting self-driving cars.

The goal is to prevent false negatives and prevent false positives, though this is not always going to be possible, thus, the system has to be adept enough to cope with those possibilities.

For a Tesla on Autopilot, it is important to realize that the existing automation is considered at Level 2 of the automated driving capabilities, meaning that it is a driver-assisted kind of automation and not fully autonomous.

For Level 2 cars, the human driver is still considered the responsible driver of the vehicle.

In the case of falsely believing that the Burger King sign was a stop sign, even if the automation tried to come to a full stop, the human driver is presumed to be in-charge and should override that kind of adverse driving action.

As I have repeatedly exhorted, we are heading into the dangerous territory of expecting human drivers to override automation in Level 2 and Level 3 rated cars, which you can bet many human drivers will not do or will do so belatedly due to a false belief that the car is soundly driving itself.

You could say that human drivers will be making false positive and false negative judgments about what their car automation is doing, any of which can then lead to dreadful calamity.

That is why some are arguing fervently that we ought to wait until the AI is good enough that we can use it in Level 4 and Level 5 self-driving cars, whereby the AI does all the driving and there is no human driving involved.

If we can get there, it would mean that the Artificial Intelligence does "know what we crave" and that consists of a safe driving journey, burgers included or not.

.

CHAPTER 14

FIREWORKS CELEBRATIONS
AND
AI SELF-DRIVING CARS

CHAPTER 14

FIREWORKS CELEBRATIONS
AND
AI SELF-DRIVING CARS

People are itching to use fireworks for this July 4th.

According to the latest reported sales figures, fireworks are selling like pancakes, hot ones packing a firecracker punch, and there is no telltale end of sales in sight (well, other than generally extinguishing after July 4th).

Why the feverish drive to obtain fireworks this year?

Several reasons are being cited.

First, most of the formal fireworks shows and events are canceled as a result of the concerns about crowds in a post-COVID setting, and thus there will not be an opportunity to witness those amazing mass displays this year.

Secondly, if large-scale events aren't in the cards, many have decided they will take matters into their own hands and put on their own fireworks show in front of their domicile.

Third, some believe that setting off fireworks is a symbolic gesture in addition to being a fun activity. This means that there is an added impetus to engage with fireworks, doing so for the sport of it and to showcase a message or notable statement about our times.

Fourth, and perhaps the most straightforward reason, after being stuck inside their homes for several months, people want to get outside and party, for which July 4th seems to offer an unbridled basis to do so.

How many times a year can you lawfully sit or stand outside your house, typically making use of the street space too, and carry on, having the time of your life and making a ruckus along with outsized noises, explosions, and razzle-dazzle flames of fire and light.

Pretty much our revered July 4th is the only time of the year to do so (well, maybe you can include New Year's Eve, but that is a lesser scaled lightweight in comparison).

And this year, July 4th lands on a Saturday, a weekend day that offers unmitigated revelry.

Many people do not quite realize that for the fireworks industry, July 4th is the time of the year wherein around 90% of their revenue occurs in a rather tightly packed two-week period. It is considered a seasonal product, usually referred to as being hyper-seasonal due to the enormous dependence on such a limited window, and the rest of the year is spent getting ready for the next such annual celebration.

Of course, there are the professional fireworks efforts that take place throughout the year. Many of the theme parks do fireworks shows year-round, while many sports make use of fireworks to herald runs scored or touchdowns made. Generally, the use of fireworks in a professional context is rather minuscule when compared to the incredible volume of public-used fireworks consumed for July 4th.

You might think that it is blatantly evident that this July 4th would be a humongous fireworks gala. Believe it or not, when the pandemic first grabbed hold in March or so, there were some predictions made that perhaps this July 4th would be a colossal dud in terms of fireworks. The assumption was that we would all be steadfastly indoors and therefore not be able to step outside to undertake the use of fireworks. This belief momentarily stalled some of the fireworks companies as they wearily wondered if they would survive as a business, given that their entire yearly income stream was perhaps about to implode.

We now know that the opposite seems to be poised to occur, namely that this will be the largest ever use of fireworks on July 4th by the general public.

Fireworks firms are heralding this moment as an astonishing lottery ticket of its time, striking gold by perchance having a product that people are demanding to obtain.

Another reason for the fireworks exuberance is the desire to do something different, other than sit around the house and play indoor games. You cannot go to the movie theatres since those are nearly all closed up, and you cannot go to the mall, and you cannot potentially even go out to eat at a restaurant.

All in all, being cooped up and after exhausting all other options, the allure of using fireworks is immensely irresistible.

There are some downsides though, which need to be pointed out, even if it seems like a spoiler for the uninhibited elation.

Being Mindful About Fireworks

One notable downside is that the sales of illegal fireworks appear to be up too.

You might be thinking that buying illegal fireworks is no big deal. Unfortunately, besides being illegal, and besides denying sales to legitimate makers of fireworks, the other perhaps non-obvious concern is that those fireworks are going to likelier cause harm.

As you know, even legal fireworks are dangerous, and people can get harmed.

Per government studies, several thousand injuries are suffered each year at this time of the year by the use of fireworks.

In one such government-run study; statistics indicate that children under the age of 15 account for over one-third of the injuries.

Sparklers and bottle rockets are some of the most frequent injury-producing products, which makes logical sense since they are often carelessly used and frequently handed over to children to tryout.

Not wanting to be gruesome, but please do realize that the most common injury is to the hands and fingers (around 28% of those with injuries), followed by the legs, eyes, and ears. Burns is the by far most common form of injury and can lead to disfigurement or outright loss of the appendage.

Thus, with illegal fireworks, you are upping the ante on potentially injuring yourself or a loved one, and keep in mind that even with legal fireworks you are still taking risks for yourself and loved ones.

Adding to the potential woes is the harm sometimes inflicted on others that have no part in your fireworks celebration. Getting a bit wild, those using fireworks on July 4th are apt to toss these explosive armaments into the air, landing on nearby neighbors, sometimes causing injury or potentially starting a fire by igniting a rooftop.

The point is that everyone and I mean everyone, needs to be thoughtful, measured, and careful in using their fireworks this coming July 4th.

Despite such high hopes, it is an easy bet that there will be lots of injuries, especially this year, due to the ramp-up of more so at-home fireworks parties and the likelihood that people will undoubtedly all want to come outside in front of their homes to see the neighborhood plethora of impromptu fireworks extravaganzas.

Emergency rooms at hospitals are already gearing up for the result.

If this seems overly doom and gloom, sorry to have cast a shadow on the merriment, but having seen firsthand the severe injuries that can occur and the long-lasting adverse impacts on a person's life, including for small children, a bit of sobriety and cautioning are worth being seen as a sour stick-in-the-mud.

Shifting gears, when people do fireworks in front of their homes, they usually opt to do so in the street.

This makes obvious sense since your front yard might have grass or shrubs, all of which are easier to catch fire, whereas the asphalt of the street is seemingly impervious to the flames and explosions caused by fireworks.

Have you ever tried to drive to the grocery store on a July 4th evening?

If you have done so, you know that it is one of the trickiest and scariest nights of the year to be driving (even harder than traversing the roadways during Halloween).

While navigating the streets in your neighborhood on July 4th, you need to slowly weave around the spots at which people have set up their fireworks displays.

Also, some people are sitting in lawn chairs on the street, and children are running back and forth, readily targets to be hit by a moving car, and of which those kids are typically so excited that they aren't looking for car traffic and are oblivious to what is occurring around them.

Nighttime darkness tends to hide what exists in and around the streets, plus the sudden flashes of fireworks can muddle your vision, distract you from looking straight ahead, and startle a driver into making a rash driving judgment.

Many a parent when asked to drive over to the store to get some more soda or chips is likely to think twice and suggest that it can wait until the next day.

Another factor involved in driving on July 4th in the nighttime is that there are idiots and (I dare say) hoodlums that relish throwing firecrackers at moving cars.

Not a good idea.

Anyone opting to drive their car during the fireworks celebratory time is taking a big chance and must have a vital reason to do so.

A related aspect is how to get a fireworks injured child or adult to the emergency room, which provides further complexity since you might drive yourself, but are limited to how fast you can go due to the obstructions and people in the streets, plus the same hurdles face any first responders driving ambulances or similar vehicles.

All told, please be safe on this coming July 4th, and if possible, stay off the roads in terms of avoid doing any driving, especially during the prime-time fireworks activities in the evening.

Mentioning the angst and throes of driving a car on July 4th brings up a related topic.

Self-driving cars are gradually going to become viable as a form of transportation. The AI-based true self-driving cars will not make use of a human driver.

Here is an intriguing question: *Will AI-based true self-driving cars have any struggle with driving during a July 4th evening and if so, what kinds of difficulties might the AI driving systems confront?*

Let's unpack the question and see.

Understanding The Levels Of Self-Driving Cars

As a clarification, true self-driving cars are ones that the AI drives the car entirely on its own and there isn't any human assistance during the driving task.

These driverless vehicles are considered a Level 4 and Level 5, while a car that requires a human driver to co-share the driving effort is usually considered at a Level 2 or Level 3. The cars that co-share the driving task are described as being semi-autonomous, and typically contain a variety of automated add-on's that are referred to as ADAS (Advanced Driver-Assistance Systems).

There is not yet a true self-driving car at Level 5, which we don't yet even know if this will be possible to achieve, and nor how long it will take to get there.

Meanwhile, the Level 4 efforts are gradually trying to get some traction by undergoing very narrow and selective public roadway trials, though there is controversy over whether this testing should be allowed per se.

Since semi-autonomous cars require a human driver, the adoption of those types of cars won't be markedly different than driving conventional vehicles, so there's not much new per se to cover about them on this topic (though, as you'll see in a moment, the points next made are generally applicable).

For semi-autonomous cars, it is important that the public needs to be forewarned about a disturbing aspect that's been arising lately, namely that despite those human drivers that keep posting videos of themselves falling asleep at the wheel of a Level 2 or Level 3 car, we all need to avoid being misled into believing that the driver can take away their attention from the driving task while driving a semi-autonomous car.

You are the responsible party for the driving actions of the vehicle, regardless of how much automation might be tossed into a Level 2 or Level 3.

Self-Driving Cars And July 4th

For Level 4 and Level 5 true self-driving vehicles, there won't be a human driver involved in the driving task.

All occupants will be passengers.

The AI is doing the driving.

Probably the most common misconception about self-driving cars is the false belief that they are going to be "superhuman" and drive in ways that are far superior to humans.

We can certainly agree that the AI will not be driving while drunk, and in that sense, yes, this is an improvement over human drivers that opt to get behind the wheel while intoxicated.

Would you though consider the act of not getting drunk to be the equivalent of "superhuman" capabilities?

Seems doubtful.

Note too that the generally accepted standard for the driving levels indicates that the AI is expected to drive in whatever manner a human driver could potentially drive on a roadway, which means that if a human can drive someplace, the AI ought to be able to do so too, though not necessarily beyond what a human can drive.

Again, that would not be especially "superhuman" as to driving.

Also, the existing levels of driving exclude the act of off-road driving. Thus, the AI might be able to do off-road driving, if the automaker and self-driving tech have such provisions, but it is not a requirement.

For a wide variety of reasons, do not set up in your mind that AI driving systems are going to be superhuman, as it is misleading and provides false expectations.

The reason that is an important point and fits this overall discussion about driving on July 4th is that you should not assume that a true self-driving car will magically drive in ways that exceed how humans would handle the driving circumstances.

Sure, the AI will not be tipsy, and it will not be "frightened" as it tries to maneuver throughout the firework's laden streets, thus avoiding those kinds of human driver foibles.

On the other hand, detecting all those low laying objects is not easy for the self-driving car.

Via the headlights of the vehicle, the cameras will be doing what they can to visually scan the scene and figure out what is taking place. Radar is going to possibly be detecting a lot of objects, though the ones close to the ground are challenging to discern. LIDAR would be helpful, as are the other sensors, though some like thermal imaging is going to get an eyeful when the fireworks are sparkling and spewing flames.

Unlike a human, the AI is unlikely to have been programmed to cope with the specifics of a July 4th phenomenon.

Humans know that there are lots of fireworks on the ground and that those are inherently dangerous. Furthermore, humans know that children are apt to be running around, sometimes even laying down or crouching in the middle of the street.

Keep in mind that today's AI lacks entirely any kind of common sense or what is referred to as common-sense reasoning. Currently, AI is very narrowly scoped and unable to "think" in the ways that humans can. This is crucial to realize since the AI is not going to "understand" what is taking place on July 4th and instead merely react to whatever happens to be seen in front of the vehicle.

A human driver would have an overarching concept of what is occurring on the roadways and be able to presumably drive more astutely via having a generalized plan of how to deal with the matters. The AI would be taking everything one step at a time, as though it had no semblance of the context of why people are in the streets and nor what they are doing.

You could argue that it doesn't matter whether a driver has a big picture perspective, and the only thing that counts is what is immediately in front of the car.

To some degree, it is the case that the action in front of the car is the most significant element, yet we also do a lot of anticipatory mental work when driving a car.

For example, I might know that the street up ahead is one that has lots of families that live in the houses bordering the roadway, and I can guess that they will be outside on July 4th in large numbers. Meanwhile, if I make a right at the end of the block, I know that there is a side street that won't likely have many people on it.

Note that via visual cues alone, you could not make that same driving judgment, and would instead have to say go straight ahead into the street that had the mass gatherings, only realizing the situation upon directly seeing it.

That's what a self-driving car is apt to do.

If you are thinking that a GPS and a map would avert this, it seems highly unlikely that any normal maps would provide a substantial clue about the aspect that the street is bounded by lots of families with small children and offer any such in-advance clues.

There is another means though that can come to play for the AI.

One aspect of self-driving cars is that they are using Machine Learning (ML) and Deep Learning (DL), a type of computational pattern matching that enables the AI to try and discover patterns.

It could be that by driving around this July 4th, the ML/DL could attempt to "learn" what the streets are like in terms of gatherings and be better prepared for next and subsequent years.

But this is probably not going to be happening this year.

Most of the self-driving tryouts are not going to be on-the-roads on July 4th, rightfully so.

The automakers and self-driving tech firms are right now coping with getting self-driving cars to safely drive in everyday circumstances. Any notion of driving in the once-a-year oddity of July 4th is considered an edge or corner case, suggesting that it is so unusual or extraordinary that it doesn't deserve attention at this time, and instead would unduly sap energy toward the standard kind of driving.

Another facet that would be difficult for the self-driving car is the potential for smoke from the fireworks to obscure what the camera sensors can see. The bright flashes of the fireworks could also impact the cameras and the nature of the visual imagery being captured and interpreted by the on-board computer system.

Conclusion

Trying to get a self-driving car to weave its way around a traditional fireworks gathering on the streets is something that goes beyond what most AI driving systems can readily accomplish today.

The AI is usually programmed to be a timid driver, moving extremely cautiously, and the number of potential objects and obstacles would undoubtedly cause the system to decide to not proceed ahead, or do so at a pace slower than a snail or a turtle.

What we need to do is add this kind of driving scenario to the list of specialized driving that we want self-driving cars to be able to eventually handle.

Meanwhile, we will be pretty much dependent upon human drivers, which as I say, ought to avoid driving on the evening of July 4th, if at all possible to so avert, and instead try to enjoy the festivities, doing so safely and determinedly not allowing anyone to get hurt.

Be safe this July 4th!

APPENDIX

APPENDIX A
TEACHING WITH THIS MATERIAL

The material in this book can be readily used either as a supplemental to other content for a class, or it can also be used as a core set of textbook material for a specialized class. Classes where this material is most likely used include any classes at the college or university level that want to augment the class by offering thought provoking and educational essays about AI and self-driving cars.

In particular, here are some aspects for class use:

o   Computer Science. Studying AI, autonomous vehicles, etc.

o   Business. Exploring technology and it adoption for business.

o   Sociology. Sociological views on the adoption and advancement of technology.

Specialized classes at the undergraduate and graduate level can also make use of this material.

For each chapter, consider whether you think the chapter provides material relevant to your course topic. There is plenty of opportunity to get the students thinking about the topic and force them to decide whether they agree or disagree with the points offered and positions taken. I would also encourage you to have the students do additional research beyond the chapter material presented (I provide next some suggested assignments they can do).

RESEARCH ASSIGNMENTS ON THESE TOPICS

Your students can find background material on these topics, doing so in various business and technical publications. I list below the top ranked AI related journals. For business publications, I would suggest the usual culprits such as the Harvard Business Review, Forbes, Fortune, WSJ, and the like.

Here are some suggestions of homework or projects that you could assign to students:

a) <u>Assignment for foundational AI research topic</u>: Research and prepare a paper and a presentation on a specific aspect of Deep AI, Machine Learning, ANN, etc. The paper should cite at least 3 reputable sources. Compare and contrast to what has been stated in this book.

b) <u>Assignment for the Self-Driving Car topic</u>: Research and prepare a paper and Self-Driving Cars. Cite at least 3 reputable sources and analyze the characterizations. Compare and contrast to what has been stated in this book.

c) <u>Assignment for a Business topic</u>: Research and prepare a paper and a presentation on businesses and advanced technology. What is hot, and what is not? Cite at least 3 reputable sources. Compare and contrast to the depictions in this book.

d) <u>Assignment to do a Startup:</u> Have the students prepare a paper about how they might startup a business in this realm. They must submit a sound Business Plan for the startup. They could also be asked to present their Business Plan and so should also have a presentation deck to coincide with it.

You can certainly adjust the aforementioned assignments to fit to your particular needs and the class structure. You'll notice that I ask for 3 reputable cited sources for the paper writing based assignments. I usually steer students toward "reputable" publications, since otherwise they will cite some oddball source that has no credentials other than that they happened to write something and post it onto the Internet. You can define "reputable" in whatever way you prefer, for example some faculty think Wikipedia is not reputable while others believe it is reputable and allow students to cite it.

The reason that I usually ask for at least 3 citations is that if the student only does one or two citations they usually settle on whatever they happened to find the fastest. By requiring three citations, it usually seems to force them to look around, explore, and end-up probably finding five or more, and then whittling it down to 3 that they will actually use.

I have not specified the length of their papers, and leave that to you to tell the students what you prefer. For each of those assignments, you could end-up with a short one to two pager, or you could do a dissertation length paper. Base the length on whatever best fits for your class, and the credit amount of the assignment within the context of the other grading metrics you'll be using for the class.

I mention in the assignments that they are to do a paper and prepare a presentation. I usually try to get students to present their work. This is a good practice for what they will do in the business world. Most of the time, they will be required to prepare an analysis and present it. If you don't have the class time or inclination to have the students present, then you can of course cut out the aspect of them putting together a presentation.

If you want to point students toward highly ranked journals in AI, here's a list of the top journals as reported by *various citation counts sources* (this list changes year to year):

- o Communications of the ACM
- o Artificial Intelligence
- o Cognitive Science
- o IEEE Transactions on Pattern Analysis and Machine Intelligence
- o Foundations and Trends in Machine Learning
- o Journal of Memory and Language
- o Cognitive Psychology
- o Neural Networks
- o IEEE Transactions on Neural Networks and Learning Systems
- o IEEE Intelligent Systems
- o Knowledge-based Systems

GUIDE TO USING THE CHAPTERS

For each of the chapters, I provide next some various ways to use the chapter material. You can assign the tasks as individual homework assignments, or the tasks can be used with team projects for the class. You can easily layout a series of assignments, such as indicating that the students are to do item "a" below for say Chapter 1, then "b" for the next chapter of the book, and so on.

a) What is the main point of the chapter and describe in your own words the significance of the topic,

b) Identify at least two aspects in the chapter that you agree with, and support your concurrence by providing at least one other outside researched item as support; make sure to explain your basis for disagreeing with the aspects,

c) Identify at least two aspects in the chapter that you disagree with, and support your disagreement by providing at least one other outside researched item as support; make sure to explain your basis for disagreeing with the aspects,

d) Find an aspect that was not covered in the chapter, doing so by conducting outside research, and then explain how that aspect ties into the chapter and what significance it brings to the topic,

e) Interview a specialist in industry about the topic of the chapter, collect from them their thoughts and opinions, and readdress the chapter by citing your source and how they compared and contrasted to the material,

f) Interview a relevant academic professor or researcher in a college or university about the topic of the chapter, collect from them their thoughts and opinions, and readdress the chapter by citing your source and how they compared and contrasted to the material,

g) Try to update a chapter by finding out the latest on the topic, and ascertain whether the issue or topic has now been solved or whether it is still being addressed, explain what you come up with.

The above are all ways in which you can get the students of your class involved in considering the material of a given chapter. You could mix things up by having one of those above assignments per each week, covering the chapters over the course of the semester or quarter.

As a reminder, here are the chapters of the book and you can select whichever chapters you find most valued for your particular class:

Chapter Title

1   Eliot Framework for AI Self-Driving Cars

2   Discovering Intelligent Life and AI Self-Driving Cars

3   Pizza Deliveries Mystery and AI Self-Driving Cars

4   Provably Beneficial AI and AI Self-Driving Cars

5   City Streets Paintings and AI Self-Driving Cars

6   Cops Shooting At Vehicles and AI Self-Driving Cars

7   US Federal Testing Log and AI Self-Driving Cars

8   Drive-By Shootings and AI Self-Driving Cars

9   AI Ethics Knobs and AI Self-Driving Cars

10 Mighty Dust Storm and AI Self-Driving Cars

11 Amazon Buys Zoox and AI Self-Driving Cars

12 Tesla With LIDAR and AI Self-Driving Cars

13 Autopilot BK Whopper and AI Self-Driving Cars

14 Fireworks Celebrations and AI Self-Driving Cars

<u>Companion Book By This Author</u>

Advances in AI and Autonomous Vehicles: Cybernetic Self-Driving Cars

Practical Advances in Artificial Intelligence (AI) and Machine Learning
by
Dr. Lance B. Eliot, MBA, PhD

<u>Chapter Title</u>

This title is available via Amazon and other book sellers

This title is available via Amazon and other book seller

Innovation and Thought Leadership on Self-Driving Driverless Cars

by Dr. Lance B. Eliot, MBA, PhD

This title is available via Amazon and other book sellers

<u>Companion Book By This Author</u>

New Advances in AI Autonomous Driverless Cars Self-Driving Cars

by Dr. Lance B. Eliot, MBA, PhD

<u>Chapter Title</u>

1 Eliot Framework for AI Self-Driving Cars

2 Self-Driving Cars Learning from Self-Driving Cars

3 Imitation as Deep Learning for Self-Driving Cars

4 Assessing Federal Regulations for Self-Driving Cars

5 Bandwagon Effect for Self-Driving Cars

6 AI Backdoor Security Holes for Self-Driving Cars

7 Debiasing of AI for Self-Driving Cars

8 Algorithmic Transparency for Self-Driving Cars

9 Motorcycle Disentanglement for Self-Driving Cars

10 Graceful Degradation Handling of Self-Driving Cars

11 AI for Home Garage Parking of Self-Driving Cars

12 Motivational AI Irrationality for Self-Driving Cars

13 Curiosity as Cognition for Self-Driving Cars

14 Automotive Recalls of Self-Driving Cars

15 Internationalizing AI for Self-Driving Cars

16 Sleeping as AI Mechanism for Self-Driving Cars

17 Car Insurance Scams and Self-Driving Cars

18 U-Turn Traversal AI for Self-Driving Cars

19 Software Neglect for Self-Driving Cars

This title is available via Amazon and other book sellers

<u>Companion Book By This Author</u>

Introduction to
Driverless Self-Driving Cars

by Dr. Lance B. Eliot, MBA, PhD

<u>Chapter Title</u>

This title is available via Amazon and other book sellers

Companion Book By This Author
Autonomous Vehicle Driverless
Self-Driving Cars and Artificial Intelligence
by Dr. Lance B. Eliot, MBA, PhD

Chapter Title

1 Eliot Framework for AI Self-Driving Cars

2 Rocket Man Drivers and AI Self-Driving Cars

3 Occam's Razor Crucial for AI Self-Driving Cars

4 Simultaneous Local/Map (SLAM) for Self-Driving Cars

5 Swarm Intelligence for AI Self-Driving Cars

6 Biomimicry and Robomimicry for Self-Driving Cars

7 Deep Compression/Pruning for AI Self-Driving Cars

8 Extra-Scenery Perception for AI Self-Driving Cars

9 Invasive Curve and AI Self-Driving Cars

10 Normalization of Deviance and AI Self-Driving Cars

11 Groupthink Dilemma for AI Self-Driving Cars

12 Induced Demand Driven by AI Self-Driving Cars

13 Compressive Sensing for AI Self-Driving Cars

14 Neural Layer Explanations for AI Self-Driving Cars

15 Self-Adapting Resiliency for AI Self-Driving Cars

16 Prisoner's Dilemma and AI Self-Driving Cars

17 Turing Test and AI Self-Driving Cars

18 Support Vector Machines for AI Self-Driving Cars

19 "Expert Systems and AI Self-Driving Cars" by Michael Eliot

This title is available via Amazon and other book sellers

<u>Companion Book By This Author</u>

Transformative Artificial Intelligence Driverless Self-Driving Cars

by Dr. Lance B. Eliot, MBA, PhD

<u>Chapter Title</u>

This title is available via Amazon and other book sellers

Companion Book By This Author

Disruptive Artificial Intelligence and Driverless Self-Driving Cars

by Dr. Lance B. Eliot, MBA, PhD

Chapter Title

This title is available via Amazon and other book sellers

<u>Companion Book By This Author</u>

State-of-the-Art
AI Driverless Self-Driving Cars

by Dr. Lance B. Eliot, MBA, PhD

<u>Chapter Title</u>

This title is available via Amazon and other book sellers

Companion Book By This Author

Top Trends in
AI Self-Driving Cars

by Dr. Lance B. Eliot, MBA, PhD

This title is available via Amazon and other book sellers

<u>Companion Book By This Author</u>

AI Innovations and Self-Driving Cars

by Dr. Lance B. Eliot, MBA, PhD

<u>Chapter Title</u>

This title is available via Amazon and other book sellers

This title is available via Amazon and other book sellers

<u>Companion Book By This Author</u>

Sociotechnical Insights and AI Driverless Cars

by Dr. Lance B. Eliot, MBA, PhD

<u>Chapter Title</u>

This title is available via Amazon and other book sellers

Pioneering Advances for AI Driverless Cars

by Dr. Lance B. Eliot, MBA, PhD

<u>Companion Book By This Author</u>

Leading Edge Trends for AI Driverless Cars

by Dr. Lance B. Eliot, MBA, PhD

<u>Chapter Title</u>

This title is available via Amazon and other book sellers

Companion Book By This Author

The Cutting Edge of AI Autonomous Cars

by Dr. Lance B. Eliot, MBA, PhD

Chapter Title

1 Eliot Framework for AI Self-Driving Cars

2 Driving Controls and AI Self-Driving Cars

3 Bug Bounty and AI Self-Driving Cars

4 Lane Splitting and AI Self-Driving Cars

5 Drunk Drivers versus AI Self-Driving Cars

6 Internal Naysayers and AI Self-Driving Cars

7 Debugging and AI Self-Driving Cars

8 Ethics Review Boards and AI Self-Driving Cars

9 Road Diets and AI Self-Driving Cars

10 Wrong Way Driving and AI Self-Driving Cars

11 World Safety Summit and AI Self-Driving Cars

This title is available via Amazon and other book sellers

Companion Book By This Author

The Next Wave of
AI Self-Driving Cars

by Dr. Lance B. Eliot, MBA, PhD

Chapter Title

This title is available via Amazon and other book sellers

Companion Book By This Author

Revolutionary Innovations of AI Self-Driving Cars

by Dr. Lance B. Eliot, MBA, PhD

Chapter Title

This title is available via Amazon and other book sellers

Companion Book By This Author

AI Self-Driving Cars
Breakthroughs

by Dr. Lance B. Eliot, MBA, PhD

This title is available via Amazon and other book sellers

Companion Book By This Author

Trailblazing Trends for
AI Self-Driving Cars

by Dr. Lance B. Eliot, MBA, PhD

Chapter Title

This title is available via Amazon and other book sellers

Companion Book By This Author

Ingenious Strides for **AI Driverless Cars**

by Dr. Lance B. Eliot, MBA, PhD

Chapter Title

This title is available via Amazon and other book sellers

This title is available via Amazon and other book sellers

Companion Book By This Author

Visionary Secrets of
AI Driverless Cars

by Dr. Lance B. Eliot, MBA, PhD

Chapter Title

This title is available via Amazon and other book sellers

Companion Book By This Author

Spearheading
AI Self-Driving Cars

by Dr. Lance B. Eliot, MBA, PhD

Chapter Title

This title is available via Amazon and other book sellers

Companion Book By This Author

Spurring
AI Self-Driving Cars

by Dr. Lance B. Eliot, MBA, PhD

This title is available via Amazon and other book sellers

Avant-Garde
AI Driverless Cars

by Dr. Lance B. Eliot, MBA, PhD

This title is available via Amazon and other book sellers

Companion Book By This Author

AI Self-Driving Cars
Evolvement

by Dr. Lance B. Eliot, MBA, PhD

Chapter Title

This title is available via Amazon and other book sellers

<u>Companion Book By This Author</u>

AI Driverless Cars
Chrysalis

by Dr. Lance B. Eliot, MBA, PhD

<u>Chapter Title</u>

1 Eliot Framework for AI Self-Driving Cars

2 Object Poses and AI Self-Driving Cars

3 Human In-The-Loop and AI Self-Driving Cars

4 Genius Shortage and AI Self-Driving Cars

5 Salvage Yards and AI Self-Driving Cars

6 Precision Scheduling and AI Self-Driving Car

7 Human Driving Extinction and AI Self-Driving Cars

This title is available via Amazon and other book sellers

<u>Companion Book By This Author</u>

Boosting
AI Autonomous Cars

by Dr. Lance B. Eliot, MBA, PhD

<u>Chapter Title</u>

This title is available via Amazon and other book sellers

This title is available via Amazon and other book sellers

<u>Companion Book By This Author</u>

AI Autonomous Cars Forefront

by Dr. Lance B. Eliot, MBA, PhD

This title is available via Amazon and other book sellers

Companion Book By This Author

AI Autonomous Cars Emergence

by Dr. Lance B. Eliot, MBA, PhD

This title is available via Amazon and other book sellers

AI Autonomous Cars Progress

by Dr. Lance B. Eliot, MBA, PhD

This title is available via Amazon and other book sellers

Dr. Lance B. Eliot

Companion Book By This Author

AI Self-Driving Cars
Prognosis

by Dr. Lance B. Eliot, MBA, PhD

This title is available via Amazon and other book sellers

<u>Companion Book By This Author</u>

AI Self-Driving Cars
Momentum

by Dr. Lance B. Eliot, MBA, PhD

<u>Chapter Title</u>

This title is available via Amazon and other book sellers

Companion Book By This Author

AI Self-Driving Cars
Headway

by Dr. Lance B. Eliot, MBA, PhD

This title is available via Amazon and other book sellers

<u>Companion Book By This Author</u>

AI Self-Driving Cars Vicissitude

by Dr. Lance B. Eliot, MBA, PhD

<u>Chapter Title</u>

This title is available via Amazon and other book sellers

Companion Book By This Author

AI Self-Driving Cars
Autonomy

by Dr. Lance B. Eliot, MBA, PhD

This title is available via Amazon and other book sellers

This title is available via Amazon and other book sellers

Companion Book By This Author

AI Driverless Cars
Potentiality

by Dr. Lance B. Eliot, MBA, PhD

Chapter Title

1 Eliot Framework for AI Self-Driving Cars

2 Russian Values and AI Self-Driving Cars

3 Friendships Uplift and AI Self-Driving Cars

4 Dogs Driving and AI Self-Driving Cars

5 Hypodermic Needles and AI Self-Driving Cars

6 Sharing Self-Driving Tech Is Not Likely

7 Uber Driver "Kidnapper" Is Self-Driving Car Lesson

8 Gender Driving Biases In AI Self-Driving Cars

9 Slain Befriended Dolphins Are Self-Driving Car Lesson

10 Analysis Of AI In Government Report

11 Mobility Frenzy and AI Self-Driving Cars

This title is available via Amazon and other book sellers

Companion Book By This Author

AI Driverless Cars
Realities

by Dr. Lance B. Eliot, MBA, PhD

Chapter Title

1   Eliot Framework for AI Self-Driving Cars

2   Non-Driving Robots and AI Self-Driving Cars

3   HealthTech and AI Self-Driving Cars

4   Rudest Drivers and AI Self-Driving Cars

5   Aliens On Earth and AI Self-Driving Cars

6   AI Human Rights and AI Self-Driving Cars

7   Pope's AI Ethics and AI Self-Driving Cars

8   Human Judgment and AI Self-Driving Cars

9   DoD AI Ethics and AI Self-Driving Cars

10   Group Dynamics and AI Self-Driving Cars

11   Medical Emergencies Inside AI Self-Driving Cars

This title is available via Amazon and other book sellers

<u>Companion Book By This Author</u>

AI Self-Driving Cars
Materiality

by Dr. Lance B. Eliot, MBA, PhD

<u>Chapter Title</u>

1 Eliot Framework for AI Self-Driving Cars

2 Baby Sea Lion and AI Self-Driving Cars

3 Traffic Lights and AI Self-Driving Cars

4 Roadway Edge Computing and AI Self-Driving Cars

5 Ground Penetrating Radar and AI Self-Driving Cars

6 Upstream Parable and AI Self-Driving Cars

7 Red-Light Auto-Stopping and Self-Driving Cars

8 Falseness of Superhuman AI Self-Driving Cars

9 Social Distancing and AI Self-Driving Cars

10 Apollo 13 Lessons and AI Self-Driving Cars

11 FutureLaw and AI Self-Driving Cars

This title is available via Amazon and other book sellers

<u>Companion Book By This Author</u>

AI Self-Driving Cars
Accordance

by Dr. Lance B. Eliot, MBA, PhD

<u>Chapter Title</u>

This title is available via Amazon and other book sellers

Companion Book By This Author

AI Self-Driving Cars
Equanimity

by Dr. Lance B. Eliot, MBA, PhD

Chapter Title

This title is available via Amazon and other book sellers

Companion Book By This Author

AI Self-Driving Cars Divulgement

by Dr. Lance B. Eliot, MBA, PhD

This title is available via Amazon and other book sellers

ABOUT THE AUTHOR

Dr. Lance B. Eliot, Ph.D., MBA is a globally recognized AI expert and thought leader, an experienced executive and leader, a successful serial entrepreneur, and a noted scholar on AI, including that his Forbes and AI Trends columns have amassed over 2.8+ million views, his books on AI are frequently ranked in the Top 10 of all-time AI books, his journal articles are widely cited, and he has developed and fielded dozens of AI systems.

He currently serves as the CEO of Techbruim, Inc. and has over twenty years of industry experience including serving as a corporate officer in billion-dollar sized firms and was a partner in a major consulting firm. He is also a successful entrepreneur having founded, ran, and sold several high-tech related businesses.

Dr. Eliot previously hosted the popular radio show *Technotrends* that was also available on American Airlines flights via their in-flight audio program, he has made appearances on CNN, has been a frequent speaker at industry conferences, and his podcasts have been downloaded over 100,000 times.

A former professor at the University of Southern California (USC), he founded and led an innovative research lab on Artificial Intelligence. He also previously served on the faculty of the University of California Los Angeles (UCLA) and was a visiting professor at other major universities. He was elected to the International Board of the Society for Information Management (SIM), a prestigious association of over 3,000 high-tech executives worldwide.

He has performed extensive community service, including serving as Senior Science Adviser to the Congressional Vice-Chair of the Congressional Committee on Science & Technology. He has served on the Board of the OC Science & Engineering Fair (OCSEF), where he is also has been a Grand Sweepstakes judge, and likewise served as a judge for the Intel International SEF (ISEF). He served as the Vice-Chair of the Association for Computing Machinery (ACM) Chapter, a prestigious association of computer scientists. Dr. Eliot has been a shark tank judge for the USC Mark Stevens Center for Innovation on start-up pitch competitions and served as a mentor for several incubators and accelerators in Silicon Valley and in Silicon Beach.

Dr. Eliot holds a Ph.D. from USC, MBA, and Bachelor's in Computer Science, and earned the CDP, CCP, CSP, CDE, and CISA certifications.

ADDENDUM

AI Self-Driving Cars Divulgement

Practical Advances in Artificial Intelligence (AI) and Machine Learning

By
Dr. Lance B. Eliot, MBA, PhD

———

For supplemental materials of this book, visit:

www.ai-selfdriving-cars.guru

For special orders of this book, contact:

LBE Press Publishing

Email: LBE.Press.Publishing@gmail.com